THE CAMBRIDGE BIBLE COMMENTARY

NEW ENGLISH BIBLE

GENERAL EDITORS

P. R. ACKROYD, A. R. C. LEANEY, J. W. PACKER

LUKE

THE
GOSPEL ACCORDING TO
LUKE

COMMENTARY BY

E. J. TINSLEY
Professor of Theology, University of Leeds

CAMBRIDGE
AT THE UNIVERSITY PRESS
1965

PUBLISHED BY
THE SYNDICS OF THE CAMBRIDGE UNIVERSITY PRESS

Bentley House, 200 Euston Road, London, N.W. 1
American Branch: 32 East 57th Street, New York 22, N.Y.
West African Office: P.O. Box 33, Ibadan, Nigeria

©

CAMBRIDGE UNIVERSITY PRESS

1965

Printed in Great Britain at the University Printing House, Cambridge
(Brooke Crutchley, University Printer)

GENERAL EDITORS' PREFACE

The aim of this series is to provide the text of the New English Bible closely linked to a commentary in which the results of modern scholarship are made available to the general reader. Teachers and young people preparing for such examinations as the General Certificate of Education at Ordinary or Advanced Level in Britain, and for similar qualifications elsewhere, have been especially kept in mind. The commentators have been asked to assume no specialized theological knowledge and no knowledge of Greek and Hebrew. Bare references to other literature and multiple references to other parts of the Bible have been avoided. Actual quotations have been given as often as possible.

Within these quite severe limits each commentator will attempt to set out the main findings of recent New Testament scholarship and to describe the historical background to the text. The main theological content of the New Testament will also be critically discussed.

Much attention has been given to the form of the volumes. The aim is to produce books each of which will be read consecutively from first to last page. The introductory material leads naturally into the text, which itself leads into the alternating sections of commentary. By this means it is hoped that each book will be easily read and remain in the mind as a unity.

The series will be prefaced by a volume—*Understanding the New Testament*—which will outline the larger historical background, say something about the growth and transmission of the text, and answer the question 'Why should we study the New Testament?' Another volume—*The New Testament Illustrated*—will contain maps, diagrams and photographs.

P. R. A.

A. R. C. L.

J. W. P.

EDITOR'S PREFACE

In the preparation of this commentary I have received invaluable help from the General Editors, and from the Cambridge University Press. This I very gratefully acknowledge.

I have of course drawn on the work of many scholars and some of my indebtedness is indicated in the note on further study at the end of the volume.

I should also like to thank my secretary, Miss Dorothy Raper, for her help in preparing the typescript, and my wife for assistance in correcting proofs.

E. J. T.

CONTENTS

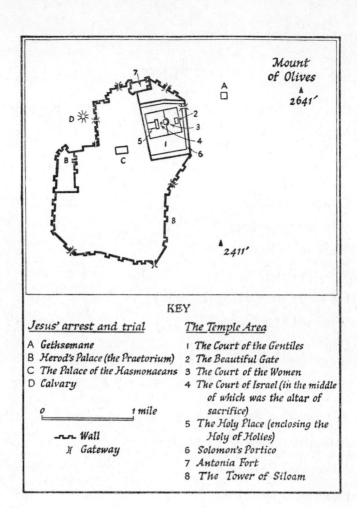

Mount
of Olives
▲
2641'

▲
2411'

PLAN OF THE TEMPLE

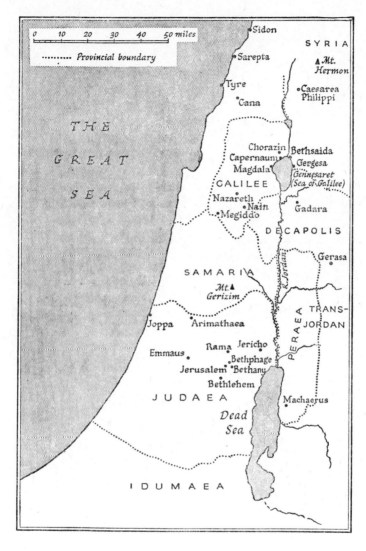

MAP OF PALESTINE

THE GOSPEL ACCORDING TO

LUKE

✳ ✳ ✳ ✳ ✳ ✳ ✳ ✳ ✳ ✳ ✳ ✳ ✳

ON READING A GOSPEL

The intelligent reading and appreciation of any book involves, among other things, finding the answers to four questions:

(1) *Who* was the author?
(2) *What* sort of a book has he written?
(3) *Why* has he written it and for whom?
(4) *When* and *where* did he write it?

All these questions, although not necessarily in this order, can be asked of Luke's Gospel. Because of the special character of the book there is more to both the questions and the answers than meets the beginner's eye.

(1) This question cannot be answered simply by giving a name and saying what is known about the life of the person concerned. The author is a Christian evangelist and we need to be clear about what such a person is.

(2) Here we ought to remember that the literary form of the book is a Gospel, a rare type of composition. Very few Christian Gospels have come down to us. There are the four in the New Testament and a number of other Gospels not in the New Testament (like the recently discovered Gospel of Thomas). A 'Gospel' is not like what a modern biography of Jesus would be, nor is it a sermon or a philosophical argument. It is a distinctive kind of writing. Further, Luke is a special kind of Gospel, because it is the only one, so far as we know, which was written as part of a two-volume work. The author intended the reading of the Gospel to be followed by a reading of Acts.

(3) It is never a simple matter to discover the motives of a writer. He may state his intentions in a preface; but any creative writer expresses more than he is consciously aware of at the time of writing. Edmund Spenser in his letter to Sir Walter Raleigh expounds 'his whole intention' in writing *The Faerie Queene*. In fact, he only completed six of the projected twelve books because once he had started, the work developed a momentum of its own which altered Spenser's original plan. We must not be surprised if readers discover meanings which may not have been in the author's mind. Language has that possibility of suggestion.

(4) The date and place of the writing of Luke's Gospel are more than bare facts. The date shows the length of the interval between the time of Jesus and the writing of the Gospel. It also shows where Luke fits into the order in which the four Gospels were written. The place where Luke was written is important if we are to see the possible influence of environment on the formation of the Gospel.

WHO WAS THE AUTHOR?

Luke has been named by church tradition as the author of this Gospel (and of the Acts of the Apostles). This tradition can be traced back as far as a prefatory note to the Gospel written in the second half of the second century A.D. This was intended to counteract the influence of Marcion, who wanted Christians to discard the Old Testament and prune the New Testament of its influence. This 'anti-Marcionite prologue', as it is called, speaks of the author as 'Luke a Syrian from Antioch', a doctor by profession, an associate of Paul till the latter's martyrdom, unmarried, and dying at the age of 84 in Boeotia, in central Greece. This source then goes on to say that he also wrote Acts. The same kind of tradition is referred to in other sources belonging to this period (e.g. the writings of Irenaeus, bishop of Lugdunum, or Lyons, and the Muratorian Canon, a second-century fragment, called after its first editor L. A.

Muratori, giving a list of the New Testament books accepted
by the church in Rome at that time). Some of the language of
the evangelist, and his attitude to certain events (like the
woman with the haemorrhages in Luke 8: 43 ff.) might well
support the tradition that he was a doctor, but what we know
of the language of the time, from contemporary documents,
suggests that any fairly well educated person would be familiar
with such terms. More important is the mention in the
tradition of Luke's association with Paul. This raises the
interesting question of the extent to which we can detect
religious attitudes and ideas similar to those in Paul's writings.

The biographical information which we can gather from
the New Testament is the same as that in church tradition.
Paul sends greetings 'from our dear friend Luke, the doctor'
(Col. 4: 14), refers to Luke as his companion: 'I have no one
with me but Luke' (2 Tim. 4: 11) and includes him in a list of
his 'fellow-workers' (Philem. 24). Some have thought that
the 'Lucius' referred to in Rom. 16: 21 and Acts 13: 1 is Luke,
but the passage in Acts makes Lucius' home country not
Antioch but a district in North Africa, Cyrene. If the 'we-
passages' in Acts (those sections in which, suddenly, the first
person 'we' is used: Acts 16: 10–17; 20: 5–15; 21: 1–18; 27: 1 —
28: 16), are from a travel diary kept by Luke, then he first
appears on the stage of history at Troas, the port of Asia Minor
(possibly identical with the Troy of Homer) from which he
and Paul set sail for Greece (Acts 16: 11).

The bare facts of the early church tradition about Luke
could have been obtained from the New Testament itself:
namely that he was a doctor and knew Paul. Other details,
for instance that Luke was the unnamed companion of
Cleopas on the walk to Emmaus (Luke 24), that he was one of
the seventy-two of Luke 10, or that he was a painter and
the first to paint Mary the mother of Jesus are pious legends
which grew up in the life of the Church.

The facts supplied by the New Testament tell us a little
about Luke's habits as an author, but they do not help us to

3

answer the profounder aspects of the question: Who was the author? The proper answer to that question sounds simple enough. He was an 'evangelist' who wrote a 'Gospel', but these frequently used words are technical Christian terms and they require careful examination.

WHAT SORT OF BOOK?

The word 'evangelist' now means a person who passionately seeks to convert at all costs, often by the use of highly personal and emotional language. This has obscured our understanding of the character and content of the first Christian evangelism. We need to remember that for the early Christians 'the Gospel' was not, in the first instance, something said *about* Jesus. It was something said *by* Jesus (believed to be the risen ascended Lord) to mankind through the Church. How this was done remained a mystery, but the first Christians saw it as the action of the Holy Spirit prompting them, in worship and in life, to discover the present reality of Christ. Paul can, on occasion, speak of 'my' Gospel, but he certainly did not mean that it was his in the sense that it was some kind of address he had put together to be used as he wished. It is Paul who is most insistent that it is not he who is preaching the Gospel, but the Lord Christ himself who is proclaiming the Gospel in his own manner through his Christians.

This means that while the Gospel is 'about' Jesus it must be about him in a way which allows him to speak for himself. The good evangelist is the one who least gets in the way of the Gospel, and this happens when he is least aware of the Gospel as *his* work. He must use a language and a method which points away from himself, and he will be confident that if he relies on the Holy Spirit this language and method will be his. From the references to the Holy Spirit in the Gospel and in Acts it seems that Luke, like John, was aware that he was activated by the Spirit in his work as an evangelist.

It is easier then to say what a Gospel is not than what it is, since it is a unique form. It is not a biography of Jesus as we normally understand biography. There are none of the personal reminiscences or character studies that we expect in a biography, although, as we shall see, Luke comes nearest, of all the evangelists, to giving us such a work. There is some of this human interest in Luke but it remains subordinate to the requirements of Gospel-writing. Nor is the Gospel an educational or propagandist work. A Gospel is not an educational handbook about Jesus which argues the case for belief in his divinity. A Gospel is nearer to preaching than to teaching. For the early Christians, one did not go from education to faith, but from faith to education (catechism). They heard the Gospel and made a first acceptance of it; then they wanted to be taught more about it. Finally a Christian Gospel is not like a modern historical reconstruction of somebody's life which aims to get at the facts. For a Christian Gospel-writer the subject of his book, Jesus of Nazareth, is not only an historical person (although he is certainly that), but a divine being in the life of Godhead itself (the Lord Christ). And when all the facts about the historical person are agreed upon and set out, the problem of faith in the divine being is by no means settled. So the Gospel-writer believes that he must write in such a way as to enable the reader to see the double meaning of Jesus. This might seem as if a Gospel-writer is necessarily a propagandist. But if we mean by propaganda going to great lengths to work on the minds and feelings of an audience, playing on fears, prejudices and anxieties, then the New Testament Gospels are not propaganda. The remarkable thing is the way the evangelists can restrain their faith, especially their Easter faith, so as to allow the events to tell their own story. This is particularly true of Mark, and to a lesser extent of Matthew, Luke and John.

An evangelist then presents the material about Jesus in such a way as to invite primarily not interest, nor information, nor admiration, but faith. Luke wants Theophilus to have 'authentic knowledge' (1: 4) in this sense. But faith is something which Theophilus, like everybody else, must come to freely in his own way. Jesus himself was scrupulous to avoid doing or saying anything which would compel belief. This is the reason for his frequent use of irony and allegory which we shall notice as we go through the Gospel. *Irony* means a situation or a saying which is deliberately ambiguous. It can have different meanings for different people, according to their standpoint. Irony makes a sharp contrast between what superficially appears to be the case and what actually is the case. An illustration of an ironic saying is Luke 15: 7 where Jesus says 'there will be greater joy in heaven over one sinner who repents than over ninety-nine righteous people who do not need to repent'. But who are these people who do not need to repent? They do not exist, for all men need to repent! Perhaps then they are those who do not *think* they need to repent. In which case there will be more rejoicing in heaven when they do repent than over anyone else. They will find themselves among the lost sheep after all! An *allegory* is a story where the situations and characters stand for something else which the reader has to identify. A good example is Jesus' parable of the vineyard in Luke 20: 9–18. Jesus' method is not to proclaim himself plainly and directly but to allow his contemporaries to feel their own way to the meaning of what he is doing and saying.

WHY HAS HE WRITTEN IT?

Such are the general aims of a New Testament evangelist. Luke's Gospel differs from the other New Testament Gospels in that it was written as the first of two volumes. There are good reasons for thinking that the Acts of the Apostles was written soon after the Gospel to complete the author's presentation of Christian beginnings. Luke, in fact, is a bridge-writer within the four Gospels. His point of view comes midway between Mark and Matthew on the one hand and John on the other. With Mark and Matthew he shares the belief that

Jesus is the mysterious 'Son of Man' whose mission is God's 'sign for the times'. For Luke also, as for John, Jesus is the 'Lord' Christ, a king who goes majestically along the way that is marked out for him by the Father, a way that culminates in ascension. He also forms a link between the tradition about what Jesus did and said, and the tradition we find in the epistles, which tell us about the life of a Christian who believes in Jesus. Both Luke and Acts give the Gospel of Jesus. In Luke it is the Gospel which is Jesus himself, in his actual person and life. In Acts it is the Gospel of Jesus proclaimed and lived by him through the action of the Holy Spirit in the lives of his followers in the Church. It looks as if the evangelist aimed at showing in both works that Jesus is the Christian Gospel, both as a unique event and as a pattern of life. The way of Christ in the Gospel is seen to be the way of the Christian in Acts. The way of Christ extends in the Gospel from the descent of the Spirit at the nativity to the ascension. The way of the Christian in Acts extends from the descent of the Spirit (at Pentecost and at baptism) to the vision of 'the glory of God, and Jesus standing at God's right hand' (Acts 7: 55). This vision of Christ at God's right hand is the inspiration for the Church to make a way for the Lord over the whole world. Hence the activity which Luke describes in Acts 8–28.

Each of the four New Testament evangelists wishes to emphasize particular features of the activity of Jesus—so much so that it is possible to give sub-titles to the Gospels. The subject of Mark is 'Jesus the hidden Messiah', of Matthew 'Jesus the royal Messiah and new Moses', and of John 'Jesus the true and only Son'. Luke's Gospel might be given the sub-title 'Jesus—a sign which men reject' (2: 34).

Luke believed that in the life and action of Jesus certain key crises in the history of Israel, when it was faced with acceptance or rejection of the call of God, were being lived over again. What was particularly at stake was whether Israel would recognize and accept as its destiny under God a mission which

7

might involve humiliation by the Gentiles even if it resulted in a universal salvation. It is very likely that Jesus himself saw things in this way. The whole ministry of Jesus faced men with a crisis, the crisis of whether to take him on faith as a sign to be accepted, or to reject him, in unbelief, as a 'scandal'. The birth of Jesus is presented alongside that of John the Baptist in such a way as to indicate that John is the last-born of the old Israel and Jesus the first-born of the new, the glory of the people of Israel (2: 32).

This is not just an interpretation of the evangelist's own. Jesus seems to have been aware that his mission, given to him by the Father and promised by the Spirit, involved at some points a reliving of important crises in Israel's history. Luke especially shows how Jesus saw his mission as a way up to Jerusalem which he must pursue in a way his Father would indicate. The temptation narratives already show the influence of the book of Deuteronomy on Jesus, and it is quite likely that it was at the back of Luke's mind when he wrote the central section of his Gospel (see note on Luke 9: 51 — 18: 30). Here Luke has so arranged his non-Marcan material as to indicate that the journey of Jesus to Jerusalem was a representation of Israel's journey to the promised land. The alternating rhythm of humiliation and glory points to the deeper theme of Luke: 'through death to the heavenly throne'. The Spirit brings about the birth of this representative of the new Israel and specially endows him at various crises in his ministry. In Jesus, Israel is faced with a perfect image of itself, carrying out in dedicated obedience the age-old mission of the people of God.

The crucial question is whether the Israel of Jesus' day will recognize this and act on it by taking him seriously. Jesus is not a sign to them by himself, in isolation. He associates his disciples with himself in a unique intimacy, so that he and they together constitute the one 'sign'. Lordship and discipleship are inseparable in Luke's thoughts, and this is one of the fundamental themes of both his books. Jesus saw that his chief temptation was like the constant temptation of old

Israel—to put God to a test of one's own rather than to trust him (see Exod. 17: 1–7). And for Luke the disciples who follow in the 'way' of Jesus will necessarily undergo the same sort of testing. The whole mission of Jesus involves a temptation to disobey. It is Luke who goes out of his way in the account of the temptation to say that the devil left Jesus not finally, but only momentarily, 'biding his time' (4: 13); later on the disciples are characterized by Jesus as those 'who have stood firmly by me in my times of trial' (22: 28). For those with eyes to see and ears to hear, suggests Luke, here is the new Moses bringing about a new and final Exodus, and here is a new Elijah bringing to completion the whole movement of Old Testament prophecy. This latter suggestion is a feature of the Gospels of Luke and John; in Mark and Matthew John the Baptist is thought of as a new-born Elijah (see note on 3: 1–20).

The modern reader may find rather strange this idea that during his ministry Jesus was enacting, at the bidding of the Father, the role of a whole nation, Israel. Here we need to remember two things: (a) The Old Testament shows the Hebrews coming to believe that the history of Israel was God's way of showing what his intentions were, not only for the Hebrews but for all men. Those who looked carefully at the history of Israel would find it to be for religion what a 'paradigm' is in the grammar of a language, a basic pattern which enables one to understand the rest. God's summons to Israel to love, obedience, humility (and suffering if need be) was his summons to all mankind. Israel (and mankind) is invited to accept this summons, confident that God will never cease to be the God of righteousness, mercy and love which he showed himself to be at decisive moments of history. The very word Israel means 'God reigns'. Already in the Old Testament this picture of Israel's role is presented in terms of a single human life in the portrait of Israel as the servant in Isa. 40–55. (b) Jesus saw himself as standing within the prophetic tradition of Israel and like many of the Old Testa-

9

ment prophets (e.g. Jeremiah, Ezekiel) he seems to have had the dramatic imagination which produced what have been called acts of 'prophetic symbolism' (like Ezekiel miming the siege of Jerusalem, Ezek. 4). These symbolic gestures were regarded by the prophets as being more than vivid illustrations. The thing being symbolized was believed to be bound up with the symbol itself. Jesus' careful planning of the entry into Jerusalem is such an act of dramatic symbolism. Other acts of this kind seem to have been the 'cleansing of the temple' (see comment on Luke 19: 45–6) and the last supper. These symbolic acts were meant to indicate that a new Israel was taking shape before the eyes of his contemporaries. God's 'paradigm' was now being given in the personal speech and action of Jesus.

It is important to notice at this point that all the titles that relate to Jesus were terms in common use both for Israel as a community and also for Israel personified in an individual human figure:

'Son of God' means Israel as a people in Hos. 11: 1 but in Ps. 2: 7 'son' means Israel personified in the king.

'Servant' is similarly used in Isa. 40–55 for both the nation of Israel and for Israel personified in the figure who appears in the 'servant' poems as, for example, Isa. 42: 1–4.

'Christ' (which means literally 'the anointed one' and so 'Messiah') is used of Israel as the anointed nation in Hab. 3: 13 ('Thou wentest forth for the salvation of thy people, for the salvation of thine anointed') and of Israel personified in the king in 1 Sam. 24: 10.

'Son of Man' is used of Israel as the 'saints of the Most High' in Dan. 7 but of an individual figure who realizes Israel's destiny in a book usually called 1 Enoch written in the period between the Old and New Testaments (roughly the last two centuries B.C.).

The old Israel of the Old Testament consisted only of those who were Jews by birth or adoption. The new Israel (the nucleus of which was Jesus and the Twelve) would

include Jews and non-Jews. This is the significance of the
mission of Jesus to which Luke gives special emphasis. In the
words of Simeon Jesus is 'a light that will be a revelation to the
heathen, and glory to thy people Israel' (Luke 2: 32).

More than the other evangelists, Luke presents Jesus as the
pattern man, and the Christian life as, through the Spirit, the
imitation of Christ. This is particularly true of Luke's treatment of the story of the passion. The New Testament as a
whole does not present the crucifixion in such a way as to
appeal primarily to our feelings, and certainly does not
exploit them. The actual sufferings of Christ are not under-
lined in the way that we might expect when we remember
that, as the New Testament itself shows, the Christian life was
practically defined (by the Pauline epistles and 1 Peter) as a
sharing in the sufferings of Christ. It is not the actual physical
(or mental) sufferings of Christ which are emphasized in the
Gospels, but the shame of Israel's rejection of her Lord.

Now while Luke shares this general perspective he does
register, more than the other evangelists, that this rejection of
Christ was a uniquely moving moment. Almost in the manner
of Greek tragic drama we find a chorus of wailing women:
'Great numbers of people followed, many women among
them, who mourned and lamented over him' (23: 27);
'the crowd who had assembled for the spectacle, when they
saw what had happened, went home beating their breasts'
(23: 48). It is Luke alone who points out, of the Son of Man,
that 'first he must endure much suffering and be repudiated
by this generation' (17: 25) and at several points in the Gospel
draws attention to Jesus as 'the man of sorrows, acquainted
with grief'. Jesus' lament over Jerusalem appears twice in
Luke's narrative (13: 34–5; 19: 41–4); on the second occasion
he is shown weeping for the tragic fate of the city. For
Luke, Jesus' ministry is a fulfilment of Old Testament
prophecy that the Christ should suffer: 'How dull you are!'
he answered. 'How slow to believe all that the prophets
said! Was the Messiah not bound to suffer thus before entering

upon his glory?' (24: 25–6). It is only in Luke that we have the explicit identification of Jesus with the *suffering* servant (Isa. 53). For Luke, suffering is a vital part of the redemptive act.

Nevertheless the note of the Lucan passion narrative is not one of pathos. If there are to be tears, says Christ, let them be tears not of pathos, which can be an indulgence, but tears of repentance for not having the moral insight and courage to see God's judgement: 'Daughters of Jerusalem, do not weep for me; no, weep for yourselves and your children. For the days are surely coming when they will say, "Happy are the barren, the wombs that never bore a child, the breasts that never fed one". Then they will start saying to the mountains, "Fall on us", and to the hills, "Cover us". For if these things are done when the wood is green, what will happen when it is dry?' (23: 28–31).

Again, Luke's narrative is characterized by references to the behaviour of Jesus during the passion. This is another characteristic which Luke shares with John. Throughout the Lucan passion Jesus acts with grandeur and serenity. There is no cry of desertion from the cross. In fact on the cross Jesus continues the ministry of forgiveness (23: 39–43) and finally makes an act of committal to the Father (23: 46).

Christ is, in Luke's Gospel and especially in the narrative of the passion, the model martyr; the martyr-disciple is the one whose life most nearly conforms to that of his Lord. The Christian life for Luke was to take up the cross day after day (9: 23); as he wrote about Simon of Cyrene carrying his cross behind Jesus he may have seen this in his mind's eye as a representation of the ideal disciple. Certainly the whole mission, speech and death of Stephen is presented in Acts in such a way as to recall the master, and the ministries of Peter and Paul are keyed to that of the master in the same kind of way. It is significant that Luke places the saying about the disciple having to imitate his Lord, *the* servant, on the occasion of the last supper (24: 26–30). This suggests that the disciples too will be involved in a reproduction of his life of service. Christ is the one and unique model for Christians. In Luke the centurion at the crucifixion calls out not, as in Mark, that this was the Son of God but—'innocent' (23: 47).

This does not mean that Luke is not interested in the death of Jesus as a means of delivering mankind from sin. It is true that he does not, like Mark and Matthew, refer to Jesus as the Son of Man who comes to give his life as 'a ransom for many'. On the other hand Luke does make striking use of the words 'salvation' and 'save', and in suggesting that the redeeming work of Jesus was not a piece of information put in so many words, but something to be *inferred* from what he did and said, the evangelist was near to the facts. Jesus seems to have been motivated by the belief, already hinted at in the Old Testament, that it was Israel's destiny under God to be humiliated by the nations in degradation, suffering and annihilation, but that this would be used by God for a saving work which would affect not only Israel but all men. A vivid character-sketch of Israel doing just this, a sketch which powerfully influenced Jesus, is to be found in the last of the 'servant-poems' of the book of Isaiah, 52: 13 — 53: 12. It looks as if Jesus saw this poem as a summons from the Father, and what he, sent to be God's Israel, must do. Perhaps Luke best represents the saving character of Jesus' work as Jesus himself saw it. And if the disciples are to follow the martyr-way of Jesus, as we see them doing in Acts, this does not mean literally doing again what he did but allowing the Spirit to shape their lives as pointers to Christ.

FOR WHOM WAS THE GOSPEL WRITTEN?

Another way of finding out why an author has written his book is to ask what sort of readers he had in mind. When we do this in the case of Luke we discover him to be an important figure in the history of Christian apologetics. 'Apologetics' is the name given to the attempt to present Christianity in a way which takes into consideration doubts, difficulties, and objections. Luke–Acts is one of the earliest *apologias* for the Christian religion. Both works are dedicated to a Gentile, Theophilus, and both are certainly intended to commend the Christian religion to people outside Judaism, and particularly to Roman readers of goodwill. For Roman readers both works have a political intention. For the author the Christian Church is the new Israel of God and he is suggesting that if the Roman authorities gave some protection to the old Israel this ought all the more to be the case for the new. The kingship of Jesus is a notable theme in Luke, but he is at pains to stress its non-political character (19: 38). In fact Luke and Acts represent the first considerable attempt to show how Church and state can live together. Luke's account of the teaching of John the Baptist exhorts state officials and soldiers to justice and honesty in such a way as to imply that they are legitimate representatives of authority and must be respected. It is Luke who pointedly presents Jesus entering Jerusalem as king, but again he implies that his kingship is non-political, signifying not imminent revolt but 'peace in heaven' (19: 38). For Luke the state, and this means the Roman state, has its proper place in the world, and must be respected and obeyed 'in all things lawful and right'. The Christian religion does not necessarily involve sedition. This is the theme of both Gospel and Acts.

Further, with Jesus and his disciples the new Israel has come. The Jews' failure to recognize this means that the old Israel is bound to become obsolescent and even perverse. In the narrative of the passion in Luke we can detect a tendency, evident in other Gospels also, to lay responsibility for the execution of Jesus firmly on the old Israel. Luke presents the Jews as guilty of political instability and prone to sedition. Their charge against Jesus ('We found this man subverting our nation, opposing the payment of taxes to Caesar, and claiming to be Messiah, a king' 23: 2), which Luke has already suggested was trumped up from casual hearsay (20: 20), is

shortly followed by their insistent clamour for the release of
Barabbas who, as the evangelist ironically points out, has
done the very things with which Jesus is charged! (23: 19, 25).
Luke implies, in both the Gospel and Acts, that the Romans
were driven to action by Jewish agitation. This is dramatically
presented in the Gospel in the threefold refusal of Pilate to
condemn Jesus (23: 3–5, 18–23).

We have already hinted that Luke is specially interested in
what must always remain a central question for Christians:
the relation between the historical Jesus and the present life
and function of the Christian Church. We need to notice now
the way this evangelist regards the teaching of Jesus. Perhaps
most people have the idea that the Christian religion equals
the teaching of Jesus, or bits of it like the Sermon on the Mount
and some parables—for example, the two sons and the good
Samaritan. They are surprised when they start reading the
Gospels. There is little of the teaching of Jesus in Mark, the
earliest; and the writers of the epistles and Revelation quote
Jesus very infrequently. To bring out Jesus' significance as
teacher seems to have been one of the reasons why Matthew
and Luke have added to the material given by Mark. And
both have done it with an eye to the role of the teaching of
Jesus in the life of the Christian community. Matthew's
Gospel is in many ways a manual for a church life based on the
law of the new Israel, the teaching of Jesus. As rules for a
community, many of the sayings of Jesus were found to be
'hard'. Hence the tendency in Matthew to allow exceptions
to the hard-and-fast rule, and the appearance of the idea of
'two standards', one for the rank and file, one for the specially
proficient. One can detect in Matthew attempts to make the
teaching of Jesus less rigorous, less ascetic in tone, in order to
produce a common rule acceptable to the majority. In Luke,
on the other hand, we seem to have the opposite tendency, a
move in a direction more rigorous and ascetic. In his account
of the rich young ruler he omits that the disciples were
astonished at Jesus' words about wealth (18: 26), and accepts

it as a general rule for all Christians that they sell their possessions (12: 33). Again in the parable of the sower it is Luke who adds that 'the pleasures of life' as such are likely to get in the way of receiving the word of God. Luke says that Jesus blessed the literally poor (6: 20) and no other Gospel has the saying 'But alas for you who are rich; you have had your time of happiness' (6: 24). And perhaps Luke believed so firmly that a rich man could not enter the kingdom of God that he dropped the references to the wealth (Matt. 27: 57) or status (Mark 15: 43) of Joseph of Arimathaea. It is not surprising therefore to find that it is Luke who appears to be the more uncompromising in his attitude to the surrender of personal ties. It is only in Luke that we have the insistence that discipleship of Jesus involves *hating* one's parents, wife and children. In a number of sayings about leaving the family for Christ, Luke uncompromisingly includes 'wife' where the other evangelists do not: Matthew has 'No man is worthy of me who cares more for father or mother than for me; no man is worthy of me who cares more for son or daughter' (10: 37). In Luke this is 'If anyone comes to me and does not hate his father and mother, wife and children, brothers and sisters, even his own life, he cannot be a disciple of mine' (14: 26). See also Mark 10: 29, Matt. 19: 29 and Luke 18: 29. After this we are not surprised to find that it is Luke who points out that James and John left *everything* to follow Jesus (5: 11) and that Levi too 'left *everything* behind' (5: 28).

WHEN AND WHERE WAS IT WRITTEN?

As we have indicated, the general outlook of this Gospel suggests from the outset that it belongs to the middle-period of Gospel-writing, between Mark and the later phase represented by John's Gospel. It seems certain that the evangelist knew Mark's Gospel and made close use of it either right from the start of his work or when he had completed a first draft. The Gospel of Luke must then be later than the period

A.D. 64–70, during which Mark appears to have been written, and probably earlier than the period A.D. 95–100 when most scholars think John's Gospel was written.

The arguments about the date of Luke's Gospel principally turn on how we interpret Luke 21: 20, 'But when you see Jerusalem encircled by armies, then you may be sure that her destruction is near'. This is either a saying of Jesus spoken *before* the fall of Jerusalem in A.D. 70 or it has been put in by the evangelist because he had lived to see this happen and believed that Jesus must have prophesied it beforehand. Many scholars reading 'encircled by armies' have believed that this decides the issue, since it must be a reference to the Roman armies of Titus, and could not have been said before the capture of Jerusalem. But Jesus saw himself as the last of the prophets of Israel (and this incidentally is a theme of Luke's Gospel: Jesus as the final Elijah). Both his manner of acting (the entry into Jerusalem, the cursing of the fig-tree) and speaking ('Verily I say unto you', 'If you have ears to hear, then hear') suggest that like the Old Testament prophets (e.g. Isa. 6), Jesus believed that he had been given a vision of the purpose of the Father ('I saw Satan as lightning falling from heaven'). He could see the destruction of Jerusalem coming with inexorable certainty. This would be one of the many moments in history when men would find themselves having to come down on one side or the other: either one took this kind of happening as a summons from God and did something about it (repented) or one took it as just another happening of no more significance than any other. It is possible to argue that the saying as Luke gives it is more likely to be what Jesus really said, and that the version in Mark's Gospel ('But when you see "the abomination of desolation" usurping a place which is not his (let the reader understand)' 13: 14) was written after the event. 'Encircled by armies' is the kind of general phrase that one expects in those prophets who see coming events, and wars in particular, as signs of the way God's judgement works. It is certainly not a phrase which clearly or undeniably points to the Roman occupation of Jerusalem in A.D. 70. If this is so, then the saying in Luke's version does not in itself suggest that it was written after A.D. 70.

Some scholars think the Gospel was written later, in A.D. 95–100. This is because there is evidence that Luke has made use of Josephus' book *The Antiquities of the Jews* which came out around A.D. 94. The suggested evidence is (*a*) Luke 3: 1 where the reference to 'Lysanias prince of Abilene' is thought to suggest that Luke misread Josephus' reference to a Lysanias who was put to death by Mark Anthony in 34 B.C.; and (*b*) that similarly Luke in Acts 5: 36–7 has confused references in Josephus to rebellions led by Theudas and Judas, getting them in the wrong order. Both points can be disputed. Archaeological finds suggest that there was a Lysanias governing Abilene at the time to which Luke refers. There were many Galilean rebellions in the first century A.D., and Theudas is an abbreviation for a number of names. Consequently, Luke may well be referring to incidents not otherwise known to us.

Precise dating of Luke's Gospel is therefore not possible, and most scholars remain content to suggest that it probably belongs to the period A.D. 75–85. We have noted the tradition that Luke died in Greece, and B. H. Streeter suggested that Corinth was probably the place where the Gospel was written. Streeter thought that the 'Theophilus' mentioned in the preface was really a disguised name for some Roman official (perhaps the Governor of Achaea whose headquarters were at Corinth) to whom Luke wished to commend both the Christian faith and Christians.

LUKE'S SOURCES OF INFORMATION

Our information about Jesus does not come direct from him. Unless what he did and said had resulted in people believing that he was divine it is not likely that we should now know very much more than has come down to us from non-Christian writers like Tacitus (A.D. 60–120), Pliny (A.D. 62–113) or Suetonius (A.D. 75–160). From them we learn simply that there was a certain Jesus who lived in the early years of the first century A.D. in Palestine, was a teacher and 'wonder-worker' and died a violent death. Outside the Christian tradition Jesus is mentioned in contemporary documents only in connexion with something else. There is no interest in him for his own sake. This information from non-Christian sources, bare as it is, is sufficient to make it difficult to hold seriously the view that there never was a Jesus. This view has had some supporters from time to time and it is still held by orthodox followers of Karl Marx.

Since our information about Jesus comes from those who believed in his divinity, the student has, right from the start, to keep his eyes open for ways in which details could have been modified, changed or omitted in the interests of faith. He should remember all the time that any Christian community, large or small, was engaged in three activities which history has since shown to have very powerful influences on the way tradition is handed down. These three activities are worship, preaching and teaching. Worship is the most conservative of these influences. People do not readily take to changes in the ways of worship to which they are accustomed, and material which has fallen into disuse elsewhere will often be found embedded in books used for worship. Preaching and teaching are, of course, notorious activities for inclining the speaker to modify his material to suit the occasion or to allow him to make his favourite point.

The study known as 'form-criticism' has shown that these influences have affected the material relating to the historical Jesus. Close analysis of the Gospels makes it clear that behind the subject-matter of these books as we now have them there is a great number of units which can be classified into types. For example, there are 'sayings-stories' which contain an important piece of the teaching of Jesus, 'miracle-stories', 'parables' and so on. These various forms show the influence, in one way or another, of the worshipping, preaching and teaching activities of the first Christian communities. Gradually, as the tradition was handed down by word of mouth, a number of individual units would be combined to illustrate some theme, like the collection of material about parables in Luke 8: 4–21. Quite early in the development of the Church the story of the passion and crucifixion seems to have been told as one unit.

The fact that the tradition about Jesus took its shape from the way Christians handed it on by word of mouth may suggest that there were no limits to the amount of elaboration and alteration that could have grown up in the course of time. Certainly in some instances historical study will show that considerable changes have taken place. Each case has to be studied on its merits in relation to all the background knowledge we have.

One factor in the three activities of worship, preaching and teaching must have had the effect of keeping the early Christians close to the facts and preventing them from being wildly led astray. This factor is specially noticeable in the writings of Luke, both the Gospel and Acts. Christ was believed to be the active force behind worship, preaching and teaching. The Gospel ends with the picture of the risen Christ in the role of what the author of Hebrews would have called their great high priest blessing the disciples. Luke seems to have seen worship as the Holy Spirit joining Christians to their risen Lord so that they can make his adoration of the Father their adoration. Again the preaching of the Christians was taken to be the means whereby the risen Christ proclaims his Gospel throughout the world till the end of time. This is certainly how Luke sees the activity of Christian preaching in Acts, and of course it is the view of Paul. In a similar way the work of the Christian teacher was not seen as an isolated activity. Through it the risen Christ was at work as the great teacher of mankind. The life and activity of Jesus of Nazareth thus shaped the pattern of these three activities, and so there is reason to believe that they were a good preservative of what actually happened.

In time some of this material was written down. The first written Christian Gospel which has survived for us is Mark. We think this because if the three Gospels Mark, Matthew and Luke are studied side by side it appears that Matthew and Luke have used Mark as one of their sources. Nearly the whole of Mark is found in Matthew and over half of it in Luke. When the passages found in all three Gospels are examined carefully there is a remarkable word for word similarity between them. This is noticeable even in the English translation; in Greek, which uses many more small words as conjunctions than English, it is unmistakable. While Matthew or Luke may sometimes differ somewhat from Mark in the way the same incident is recorded, it hardly ever happens that Matthew and Luke together differ markedly in their wording of an incident from what is found in Mark. This suggests that Mark came first and was used as a source by Matthew and Luke. This opinion is strengthened by noticing the numerous instances where Mark's version of an event has been considerably modified by one or both of the other two evangelists. An examination of these modifications suggests that Mark's is the earlier record and has been changed by the later writers to meet difficulties felt by some Christians. One example is Luke's omission of the cry of desertion on the cross 'My God, my God, why hast thou forsaken me?' which Mark has in 15: 34. Luke's Gospel represents the feelings of later Christians; they felt that Jesus could not have thought that God had forsaken him if he were the Jesus in whom they believed. As things have turned out, most Christians would make this cry from the cross the king-pin of their faith, because it implies that Jesus really experienced the whole range of human uncertainties, even the sense of the absence of God.

Luke has clearly made use of Mark as one of his sources. He has also used other information. There is a fair amount of material, consisting mostly but not exclusively of sayings of Jesus, which is found only in Matthew and Luke. Practically the whole of Luke 11 is an example. So closely similar is the wording of such passages that most scholars have assumed that those parallel versions found in Matthew and Luke, but not in Mark, must have been part of some record of the teaching of Jesus which has not survived. This lost record has been called Q. Until quite recently the most common view was that Luke made use of Q (thought to have been compiled even earlier than Mark) together with Mark. This does not account for the whole of Luke's Gospel. There are the stories in chapters 1 and 2 and, for instance, many well-known parables, like that of the two sons in 15: 11–32, which are found only in Luke. Clearly he had access to yet other sources of information. There is a theory that Luke wrote a first draft of his Gospel consisting of Q and the material which is found only in Luke and then later on, when he happened to read Mark, enlarged what he had written by inserting sections from Mark where he thought them appropriate. This theory attempted to account for the fact that in Luke the passages from Q and from Mark occur in alternate sections and are not worked together in the way they are in Matthew. Recently, however, some critics have come to doubt whether there ever was a Q. They think that the above features of Luke's Gospel can best be explained by supposing that both Mark and Matthew were among the 'many writers' the evangelist refers to in the preface. What used to be thought of as Q material in Luke is, on this theory, explained as Luke's version of material (sometimes left as it was, sometimes altered) which he found in Matthew.

There is no easy solution to these problems. The reader can only decide for himself when he has become very familiar with the language, habits and outlook of each individual gospel: Mark, Matthew and Luke.

✻   ✻   ✻   ✻   ✻   ✻   ✻   ✻   ✻   ✻   ✻   ✻   ✻

AUTHOR'S PREFACE

THE AUTHOR TO THEOPHILUS: Many writers have **1**
undertaken to draw up an account of the events that
have happened among us, following the traditions handed **2**
down to us by the original eyewitnesses and servants of
the Gospel. And so I in my turn, your Excellency, as one **3**
who has gone over the whole course of these events in
detail, have decided to write a connected narrative for
you, so as to give you authentic knowledge about the **4**
matters of which you have been informed.

✻ The fact that Luke's two volumes, the Gospel and Acts,
begin in a similar way indicates that he intended these two
books to be read as a single work. At the beginning of the
Gospel he says that he intends to confirm that the facts about
Jesus which Theophilus already knows are reliable. He also
acknowledges that he is not the first in the field; he knows of
many writers who have written about Jesus. Among these
were Mark and possibly Matthew. The new thing about Luke's
design was the attempt to show that the mission of Jesus was
the first and crucial stage of an operation by the Holy Spirit
which was now moving into a second phase in the life and
mission of the Church. Theophilus (literally the word means
'friend of God') may have been a Roman official known to
Luke. He addresses him as *Your Excellency*, a title which in
Acts he uses of a Roman governor (23: 26). ✻

The Coming of the Messiah

GOD'S WORD TO ZECHARIAH

5 IN THE DAYS of Herod king of Judaea there was a priest named Zechariah, of the division of the priesthood called after Abijah. His wife also was of priestly
6 descent; her name was Elizabeth. Both of them were upright and devout, blamelessly observing all the
7 commandments and ordinances of the Lord. But they had no children, for Elizabeth was barren, and both were well on in years.

8   Once, when it was the turn of his division and he was
9 there to take part in divine service, it fell to his lot, by priestly custom, to enter the sanctuary of the Lord and
10 offer the incense; and the whole congregation was at prayer outside. It was the hour of the incense-offering.
11 There appeared to him an angel of the Lord, standing on
12 the right of the altar of incense. At this sight, Zechariah
13 was startled, and fear overcame him. But the angel said to him, 'Do not be afraid, Zechariah; your prayer has been heard: your wife Elizabeth will bear you a son, and
14 you shall name him John. Your heart will thrill with
15 joy and many will be glad that he was born; for he will be great in the eyes of the Lord. He shall never touch wine or strong drink. From his very birth he will be
16 filled with the Holy Spirit; and he will bring back many
17 Israelites to the Lord their God. He will go before him as forerunner, possessed by the spirit and power of Elijah, to reconcile father and child, to convert the

24

rebellious to the ways of the righteous, to prepare a people that shall be fit for the Lord.'

Zechariah said to the angel, 'How can I be sure of this? 18 I am an old man and my wife is well on in years.'

The angel replied, 'I am Gabriel; I stand in attendance 19 upon God, and I have been sent to speak to you and bring you this good news. But now listen: you will lose 20 your powers of speech, and remain silent until the day when these things happen to you, because you have not believed me, though at their proper time my words will be proved true.'

Meanwhile the people were waiting for Zechariah, 21 surprised that he was staying so long inside. When he did 22 come out he could not speak to them, and they realized that he had had a vision in the sanctuary. He stood there making signs to them, and remained dumb.

When his period of duty was completed Zechariah 23 returned home. After this his wife Elizabeth conceived, 24 and for five months she lived in seclusion, thinking, 'This 25 is the Lord's doing; now at last he has deigned to take away my reproach among men.'

✶ Both Luke and John seem to have been intent on getting clear in the reader's mind what they regard as the true relation between John the Baptist and Jesus. Both agree that while John the Baptist came before Jesus in time he ranks after Jesus in importance. God is at work in the coming of both John and Jesus, although in different ways. Luke intends us to register this right at the start, and so he writes the annunciations and nativities of John and Jesus in parallel. The nativity, circumcision and 'epiphany' (public appearance) of John who 'became strong in spirit' (1: 80) is paralleled by the nativity, circumcision and 'epiphany' of Jesus who 'grew big and strong and full of wisdom' (2: 40).

5. *Herod King of Judaea*, usually referred to as 'Herod the Great', ruled from 40 B.C. to 4 B.C. For interesting background reading see S. Perowne, *The Life and Times of Herod the Great*.

the division of the priesthood called after Abijah. Priests of the Jerusalem temple had periods of duty allotted to them, decided upon by drawing lots, rather like the periods of 'residence' assigned to canons in cathedrals. Zechariah's division was called after Abijah (1 Chron. 24: 10).

10. The offering of incense, as an act of devotion, took place every morning and evening (Ps. 141: 2, 'Let my prayer be set forth as incense before thee; The lifting up of my hands as the evening sacrifice').

11. *an angel*. There is a tendency in Luke's Gospel to present religious experiences in a tangible visible way. The descent of the spirit at the baptism of Jesus is 'in bodily form' and on the Mount of Olives there is 'an angel from heaven bringing him strength'. Angels figure prominently in Acts. The ancient world believed in the existence of invisible forces of good and evil. There were good angels and evil spirits. Belief in angelic beings seems to have developed among the Jews after the exile (586 B.C.). One of the reasons for this was that the picture of angels surrounding the throne of God helped to fix the mind on the glory of a God who was beyond human imagination and thought.

15. *He shall never touch wine or strong drink*. Abstention from wine in the Old Testament was a mark not of what we should now call 'teetotalism', but of a prophetic protest against a sophisticated civilization which had forgotten God. Some people in the Old Testament (Nazirites, Rechabites) saw the vine (and its product wine) as a symbol of Israel's desertion of God. Israel in the desert where there was no vine or pomegranate (Jer. 2: 2) had been loyal to God, but in Canaan, the land of vines and olives (Deut. 8: 8),

Israel became unfaithful to God. John the Baptist is in the line of those prophets who summoned Israel to its first loyalty.

17. *possessed by the spirit and power of Elijah.* It had become a tradition in late Judaism that before the coming of the Messiah himself there would appear an Elijah figure to summon Israel to repentance (Mal. 4: 5). Here *John* is identified as the Elijah. But in the body of the Gospel Luke sees *Jesus* as being a kind of Elijah, for he is the culmination of the Old Testament prophetic movement.

25. *'my reproach among men'.* To have no children was regarded in the Old Testament not only as a misfortune but also as a social and religious disgrace, the latter because one would not be able to expect the Messiah to be amongst one's descendants. The idea that not to be able to have a child is a social and personal disgrace has unfortunately lingered on, partly no doubt because of the place of the idea in the Old Testament. Such an idea, of course, is quite irrational. ✻

GOD'S WORD TO MARY

In the sixth month the angel Gabriel was sent from God 26 to a town in Galilee called Nazareth, with a message for a 27 girl betrothed to a man named Joseph, a descendant of David; the girl's name was Mary. The angel went in and 28 said to her, 'Greetings, most favoured one! The Lord is with you.' But she was deeply troubled by what he 29 said and wondered what this greeting might mean. Then 30 the angel said to her, 'Do not be afraid, Mary, for God has been gracious to you; you shall conceive and bear a 31 son, and you shall give him the name Jesus. He will be 32 great; he will bear the title "Son of the Most High"; the Lord God will give him the throne of his ancestor David, and he will be king over Israel for ever; his reign shall 33

34 never end.' 'How can this be,' said Mary, 'when I have
35 no husband?' The angel answered, 'The Holy Spirit
will come upon you, and the power of the Most High
will overshadow you; and for that reason the holy child
36 to be born will be called "Son of God". Moreover your
kinswoman Elizabeth has herself conceived a son in her
old age; and she who is reputed barren is now in her sixth
37,38 month, for God's promises can never fail.' 'Here am I,'
said Mary; 'I am the Lord's servant; as you have spoken,
so be it.' Then the angel left her.

39   About this time Mary set out and went straight to a
40 town in the uplands of Judah. She went into Zechariah's
41 house and greeted Elizabeth. And when Elizabeth heard
Mary's greeting, the baby stirred in her womb. Then
42 Elizabeth was filled with the Holy Spirit and cried aloud,
'God's blessing is on you above all women, and his
43 blessing is on the fruit of your womb. Who am I, that the
44 mother of my Lord should visit me? I tell you, when your
greeting sounded in my ears, the baby in my womb leapt
45 for joy. How happy is she who has had faith that the
Lord's promise would be fulfilled!'

46   And Mary said:

'Tell out, my soul, the greatness of the Lord,
47   rejoice, rejoice, my spirit, in God my saviour;
48   so tenderly has he looked upon his servant,
        humble as she is.
     For, from this day forth,
     all generations will count me blessed,
49   so wonderfully has he dealt with me,
        the Lord, the Mighty One.

His name is Holy;
his mercy sure from generation to generation   50
     toward those who fear him;
the deeds his own right arm has done   51
     disclose his might:
the arrogant of heart and mind he has put to rout,
he has torn imperial powers from their thrones,   52
     but the humble have been lifted high.
The hungry he has satisfied with good things,   53
     the rich sent empty away.

He has ranged himself at the side of Israel his servant; 54
     firm in his promise to our forefathers,   55
he has not forgotten to show mercy to Abraham
     and his children's children, for ever.'

Mary stayed with her about three months and then 56
returned home.

* It has been assumed that Luke believed in the virgin birth
of Jesus. This is supported by verses 34–5, and 3: 23 where
Jesus is spoken of as 'the son, as people thought, of Joseph'.
The matter is not as precise as many have thought. Mary's
question in verse 34, *How can this be, when I have no husband?*
shows a surprise which is bewildering when one remembers
that she was betrothed to Joseph and could therefore expect
to have a son in due course. The matter is complicated by the
fact that one manuscript omits *How can this be when I have no
husband?* and reads instead *Here am I, I am the Lord's servant*, now
found in verse 38. As it stands, verse 35 about the action of the
Holy Spirit is meant to convey to the reader, by its echo of the
Genesis account of the Spirit of God at creation, that in the
birth of Jesus there is a new creative act of God, just as much
an act of God as creation itself.

29

From the beginning of the second century A.D. it has been the tradition of the Christian Church that Jesus was conceived in the womb of Mary without a human father. Many Christians have found it difficult to accept this belief for the following reasons:

(1) Belief in the virgin birth is directly referred to only in the birth narrative of Matthew and Luke and not elsewhere in the New Testament. This means that it was possible for Paul, for instance, to proclaim the Christian faith without basing it on the virgin birth.

(2) Already in pre-Christian Judaism there is evidence that speculation about what was involved in the 'Fall' of man had reached the notion that man's 'fallenness' was symbolized by sexual intercourse which therefore was felt to be sinful. The sin of Adam and Eve in Genesis 3 had come to be interpreted in a sexual sense, and sexual intercourse was held to be the means whereby the infection of original sin was passed on in the human race. This was of course one of the reasons for the later idea that the unmarried state was superior to the married.

Behind belief in the virgin birth there may therefore sometimes have been the idea that an incarnation through the male–female relationship would be unseemly. Hence belief in Jesus' birth from a virgin may have been prompted by a reverential wish to safeguard the idea of his sinlessness. Many Christians today would want to say that an incarnation through the married relationship was in one way more in keeping with God's way of revealing himself. This is by using ordinary events and real persons, at the same time leaving it possible for a non-religious interpretation of his actions to be given.

Whichever view we take, we ought to remember that the actual details of the manner of incarnation are God's secret just as much as the actual manner of resurrection is. Belief in the virgin birth is one way of doing homage to the greater thing—the incarnation.

39–45. This treatment of the meeting of Mary and Elizabeth illustrates the point already made (see pp. 6f.) that Luke's outlook seems to be midway between that of the other two Synoptic Gospels (see p. 213) and John. As in John's Gospel the Baptist in Luke is more a witness to Christ than an Elijah figure. Here, in a way reminiscent of the Old Testament prophetical tradition, the Baptist's destiny is to acknowledge Christ even before birth, and John's mother with prophetic insight acknowledges Mary as the mother of her Lord.

46–55. This song, generally known as the 'Magnificat' (in Latin the first verse is 'magnificat anima mea Dominum') is sung between the reading of the Old and New Testament lessons at Anglican Evensong. In it there are a number of important echoes of the Old Testament. Luke has composed it to suggest to the reader that the real significance of Jesus is that he embodied in himself the mission of the old Israel. It reminds one straight away of the song of Hannah after the birth of Samuel in 1 Sam. 2: 1–10. The evangelist sees Mary as a new Hannah. Just as Hannah was one of the model mothers of the old Israel, Mary is the true mother of the new Israel. Other Old Testament allusions in the song are (words similar to Luke's song are in italics):

verse 48 suggests 'Leah said, Happy am I! for *the daughters will call me happy*' (Gen. 30: 13);

verse 49 suggests 'He hath sent redemption unto his people; He hath commanded his covenant for ever:
Holy and reverend is his name' (Ps. 111: 9);

verse 50 suggests '*But the mercy of the Lord is from everlasting to everlasting upon them that fear him*' (Ps. 103: 17);

verse 51 suggests '*Thou hast scattered thine enemies with the arm of thy strength*' (Ps. 89: 10);

verse 53 suggests 'For he satisfieth the longing soul,
And the hungry soul he filleth with good' (Ps. 107: 9);

verses 54–5 suggest '*He hath remembered his mercy* and his faithfulness *toward the house of Israel*' (Ps. 98: 3).

The Magnificat therefore reads like a triumph-song of Israel (frequently pictured in the Old Testament as Mother

Zion, e.g. Isa. 51: 1–12) rejoicing at the birth of the greatest
of her sons who will bring in what was promised to Abraham.
Here is one of the places where we notice how near Luke
is to the outlook of John. In the latter's Gospel the mother of
Jesus is also seen as a symbol of Israel: at Cana-in-Galilee in
John 2: 1–11 and at the crucifixion in John 19: 25–7.

Some manuscripts read Elizabeth in verse 46 instead
of Mary. The translators of the N.E.B. suggest that
originally there may have been simply—'And she said'. In
its context this would mean Elizabeth who is the speaker in
the immediately preceding verses. The reading 'Elizabeth'
may have originated in an attempt to make this clear. There
can be no doubt, as we have just seen, that Luke intended the
speaker to be Mary the mother of Jesus. ✳

THE BIRTH OF JOHN THE BAPTIST

57 Now the time came for Elizabeth's child to be born, and
58 she gave birth to a son. When her neighbours and relatives
heard what great favour the Lord had shown her, they
59 were as delighted as she was. Then on the eighth day
they came to circumcise the child; and they were going
60 to name him Zechariah after his father. But his mother
61 spoke up and said, 'No! he is to be called John.' 'But',
they said, 'there is nobody in your family who has that
62 name.' They inquired of his father by signs what he
63 would like him to be called. He asked for a writing-
tablet and to the astonishment of all wrote down, 'His
64 name is John.' Immediately his lips and tongue were
65 freed and he began to speak, praising God. All the neighbours were struck with awe, and everywhere in the
uplands of Judaea the whole story became common talk.
66 All who heard it were deeply impressed and said, 'What

will this child become?' For indeed the hand of the
Lord was upon him.

And Zechariah his father was filled with the Holy 67
Spirit and uttered this prophecy:

'Praise to the God of Israel!   68
For he has turned to his people, saved them and set them
        free,
and has raised up a deliverer of victorious power   69
        from the house of his servant David.

So he promised: age after age he proclaimed   70
        by the lips of his holy prophets,
that he would deliver us from our enemies,   71
        out of the hands of all who hate us;
that he would deal mercifully with our fathers,   72
        calling to mind his solemn covenant.

Such was the oath he swore to our father Abraham,   73
        to rescue us from enemy hands,   74
and grant us, free from fear, to worship him
        with a holy worship, with uprightness of heart,   75
        in his presence, our whole life long.

And you, my child, you shall be called Prophet of the 76
        Highest,
for you will be the Lord's forerunner, to prepare his way
        and lead his people to salvation through knowledge 77
        of him,
        by the forgiveness of their sins:
for in the tender compassion of our God   78
        the morning sun from heaven will rise upon us,

79 to shine on those who live in darkness, under the cloud of
death,
and to guide our feet into the way of peace.'

80   As the child grew up he became strong in spirit; he
lived out in the wilds until the day when he appeared
publicly before Israel.

✽ 59. Circumcision has come to be especially associated with
Judaism but it is an ancient practice, examples of which can
be found among the Egyptians. Originally it seems to have
been some kind of initiation rite symbolizing a young boy's
entry into manhood. Among the Jews it was given a new
significance as a symbol of their covenant relation with God.
It occupies in Judaism the place Christians give to baptism.

67. Luke's work, both in the Gospel and Acts, is punctuated
at major points by references to the work of the Holy Spirit.
His theme in both works is the work of the Holy Spirit, first
in the ministry of Jesus and then in the church of Jesus.

68–79. This poem, sung as the 'Benedictus' in Anglican
Mattins, seems to have been composed by the evangelist as a
companion piece to the song of Mary in verses 46–56. There
is the same use of Old Testament language. In fact in many
cases Luke has used one half of a verse from the psalms in the
'Magnificat' and the other half here in the 'Benedictus'.
The more important Old Testament allusions are given in
italics in the following:
verse 68 suggests '*Blessed be the Lord, the God of Israel*'
(Ps. 41: 13),
    '*He hath sent redemption unto his people*' (Ps. 111: 9);
verse 69 suggests '... *will I make the horn of David to bud*'
(Ps. 132: 17). A literal translation of Luke 1: 69 would
be 'And he has raised up a horn of salvation for us in the
house of David his servant';
verses 70–2 suggest '*And he saved them from the hand* of him
that hated them,

34

> *And redeemed them from the hand of the enemy . . .*
> *And he remembered for them his covenant,*
> And repented according to *the multitude of his*
>   *mercies*' (Ps. 106: 10, 45);

verses 73–5 suggest 'For he remembered *his holy word,*
  And *Abraham his servant*' (Ps. 105: 42);

verse 76 suggests '*Prepare* ye in the wilderness *the way of the*
  Lord, make straight in the desert a high way for our
  God' (Isa. 40: 3);

verse 79 suggests '*Such as sat in darkness and in the shadow of*
  death' (Ps. 107: 10).

The subject of Zechariah's song is thus the same as Mary's:
the great day for Israel which the coming of Jesus makes.
John the Baptist is referred to only in verses 76–7 and is
presented as the *Prophet of the Highest.* When Luke comes to
record the work of John he describes it in a way which
suggests the Old Testament prophets: 'the word of God
came to John' (3: 2). ✳

THE BIRTH OF JESUS

In those days a decree was issued by the Emperor Augustus **2**
for a general registration throughout the Roman world.
This was the first registration of its kind; it took place ₂
when Quirinius was governor of Syria. For this purpose ₃
everyone made his way to his own town; and so Joseph ₄
went up to Judaea from the town of Nazareth in Galilee,
to be registered at the city of David, called Bethlehem, ₅
because he was of the house of David by descent; and
with him went Mary who was betrothed to him. She was
pregnant, and while they were there the time came for her ₆
child to be born, and she gave birth to a son, her first- ₇
born. She wrapped him round, and laid him in a manger,
because there was no room for them to lodge in the house.

8 Now in this same district there were shepherds out in the fields, keeping watch through the night over their
9 flock, when suddenly there stood before them an angel of the Lord, and the splendour of the Lord shone round
10 them. They were terror-struck, but the angel said, 'Do not be afraid; I have good news for you: there is great
11 joy coming to the whole people. Today in the city of David a deliverer has been born to you—the Messiah,
12 the Lord. And this is your sign: you will find a baby
13 lying all wrapped up, in a manger.' All at once there was with the angel a great company of the heavenly host, singing the praises of God:

14   'Glory to God in highest heaven,
     And on earth his peace for men on whom his favour rests.'

15 After the angels had left them and gone into heaven the shepherds said to one another, 'Come, we must go straight to Bethlehem and see this thing that has happened,
16 which the Lord has made known to us.' So they went with all speed and found their way to Mary and Joseph;
17 and the baby was lying in the manger. When they saw him, they recounted what they had been told about this
18 child; and all who heard were astonished at what the
19 shepherds said. But Mary treasured up all these things
20 and pondered over them. Meanwhile the shepherds returned glorifying and praising God for what they had heard and seen; it had all happened as they had been told.
21 Eight days later the time came to circumcise him, and he was given the name Jesus, the name given by the angel before he was conceived.

* Another of Luke's sections which give in miniature the significance of the whole Gospel, indeed of the whole work Luke–Acts. Like John, Luke sees the coming of Jesus as something which affects the whole of humanity, hence the startling reference to a decree of the emperor. Like John also Luke suggests to the reader that Jesus is destined to be an outsider among his own who 'would not receive him' (John 1: 11). In Luke the shepherds who recognize the 'signs' of Jesus (all that 'they had heard and seen', verse 20) are contrasted with the official 'shepherds' of Israel—the Pharisees and lawyers.

1–5. These verses raise the difficult question: where was Jesus actually born: Nazareth or Bethlehem? During his ministry Jesus is spoken of as 'Jesus of Nazareth' but in Matthew and Luke his birthplace is given as Bethlehem. There are a number of difficulties in the Lucan story. The reason he gives for Jesus being born in Bethlehem (which is seventy miles south of Nazareth his home town if Bethlehem in Judaea is meant and 2: 4 shows that it is) is that a census ordered by the Governor of Syria, Quirinius, required his parents to go to the place where Joseph's ancestor David (1: 27) had lived generations before. There was a census carried out by a Quirinius, Roman legate of Syria, but it was during the years of his rule in A.D. 6–9, which is ten years later than the date Luke has in mind—before the death of Herod in 4 B.C. (Luke 1: 5). Historians have thought it unlikely that the Roman emperor would have ordered a census in territory that was technically independent in Herod's time, and even more unlikely that he would order a census which required the population to be registered in the place where their ancestors had lived.

There may well have been some kind of census in which Joseph and Mary were involved and Luke has got the dates wrong. The story as we now have it of Joseph taking his wife who was advanced in pregnancy on such a journey may well have been influenced by the well-known prophecy in Micah

5: 2 that the Messiah would be born in Bethlehem: 'But thou, Beth-lehem Ephrathah, which art little to be among the thousands of Judah, out of thee shall one come forth unto me that is to be ruler in Israel'. Significantly Matthew makes use of this prophecy to indicate Bethlehem as Jesus' birthplace.

8–20. This passage presents in dramatic pictorial form one of the major themes of Luke's Gospel: suddenly when men are doing their ordinary work they find themselves in the presence of God. Luke intends the reader to see the shepherds as representatives of believers who are humble enough to recognize the 'signs' which God gives and are ready to act on them. The sign given is something quite ordinary: *a baby lying all wrapped up, in a manger* (verse 12) but their readiness to act on such a sign means that they find salvation. What this salvation is forms the subject of the song of the angels—peace. Peace in the thought of the Bible means more than the absence of strife. It is entire harmony of life, something which, in its perfection, only God has. But the good news of the Gospel is that God intends human beings to have a life similar to his in its freedom and satisfaction. The meaning of the angels' song is not that men can bring about peace with God or with themselves purely by their own endeavours. God's peace is God's alone, and it is his *favour* to men to bring about in them a peace which has some resemblance to his own. ✻

EARLY DAYS IN JERUSALEM

22 Then, after their purification had been completed in accordance with the Law of Moses, they brought him up
23 to Jerusalem to present him to the Lord (as prescribed in the law of the Lord: 'Every first-born male shall be
24 deemed to belong to the Lord'), and also to make the offering as stated in the law of the Lord: 'A pair of turtle doves or two young pigeons.'

There was at that time in Jerusalem a man called 25
Simeon. This man was upright and devout, one who
watched and waited for the restoration of Israel, and the
Holy Spirit was upon him. It had been disclosed to him 26
by the Holy Spirit that he would not see death until he
had seen the Lord's Messiah. Guided by the Spirit he 27
came into the temple; and when the parents brought in
the child Jesus to do for him what was customary under
the Law, he took him in his arms, praised God, and said: 28

'This day, Master, thou givest thy servant his discharge in 29
    peace;
  now thy promise is fulfilled.
For I have seen with my own eyes   30
the deliverance which thou hast made ready in full view 31
    of all the nations:
A light that will be a revelation to the heathen,   32
    and glory to thy people Israel.'

The child's father and mother were full of wonder at 33
what was being said about him. Simeon blessed them and 34
said to Mary his mother, 'This child is destined to be a
sign which men reject; and you too shall be pierced to 35
the heart. Many in Israel will stand or fall because of
him, and thus the secret thoughts of many will be laid
bare.'

There was also a prophetess, Anna the daughter of 36
Phanuel, of the tribe of Asher. She was a very old
woman, who had lived seven years with her husband after
she was first married, and then alone as a widow to 37
the age of eighty-four. She never left the temple, but
worshipped day and night, fasting and praying. Coming 38

up at that very moment, she returned thanks to God; and she talked about the child to all who were looking for the liberation of Jerusalem.

39 When they had done everything prescribed in the law of the Lord, they returned to Galilee to their own town 40 of Nazareth. The child grew big and strong and full of wisdom; and God's favour was upon him.

41 Now it was the practice of his parents to go to Jerusalem 42 every year for the Passover festival; and when he was 43 twelve, they made the pilgrimage as usual. When the festive season was over and they started for home, the boy Jesus stayed behind in Jerusalem. His parents did not 44 know of this; but thinking that he was with the party they journeyed on for a whole day, and only then did they begin looking for him among their friends and relations. 45 As they could not find him they returned to Jerusalem 46 to look for him; and after three days they found him sitting in the temple surrounded by the teachers, listening 47 to them and putting questions; and all who heard him were amazed at his intelligence and the answers he gave. 48 His parents were astonished to see him there, and his mother said to him, 'My son, why have you treated us like this? Your father and I have been searching for you 49 in great anxiety.' 'What made you search?' he said. 'Did you not know that I was bound to be in my Father's 50 house?' But they did not understand what he meant. 51 Then he went back with them to Nazareth, and continued to be under their authority; his mother treasured up all 52 these things in her heart. As Jesus grew up he advanced in wisdom and in favour with God and men.

* 22–4. Menstruation and childbirth are surrounded by ritual taboos amongst primitive peoples. The reference here is to the rites specified in Lev. 12: 1–8 where the idea seems to be that such actions were necessary because the woman had been in contact with a mysterious divine power. It is a pity that the use of the word *purification* has suggested the notion that sexual processes are necessarily unseemly. Significantly in this passage the majority of manuscripts have 'their' *purification* so as to reduce the direct reference to the mother of Jesus needing purification made in those manuscripts which read 'her' *purification*.

25–35. Another section in which the evangelist gives in broad summary the meaning of the Gospel he is about to narrate. Simeon as *one who watched and waited for the restoration of Israel* represents the Old Testament which must now make way for the New. Enlightened by the Holy Spirit Simeon is enabled to point to further significant things that Jesus will do. The mission of Jesus will be of significance both for Israel and the world (verse 32), it will be a 'sign' over which many will 'stumble', and so find themselves under judgement one way or the other (verse 35).

41–52. This episode suggests that from an early period Jesus was aware of a unique relationship with the Father. Already he shows himself feeling an obligation to carry out his Father's commands. At the baptism he is finally aware of unique sonship. *

JOHN THE BAPTIST

In the fifteenth year of the Emperor Tiberius, when **3** Pontius Pilate was governor of Judaea, when Herod was prince of Galilee, his brother Philip prince of Ituraea and Trachonitis, and Lysanias prince of Abilene, during the 2 high-priesthood of Annas and Caiaphas, the word of God came to John son of Zechariah in the wilderness. And 3

he went all over the Jordan valley proclaiming a baptism
4 in token of repentance for the forgiveness of sins, as it is
written in the book of the prophecies of Isaiah:

> 'A voice crying aloud in the wilderness,
>   "Prepare a way for the Lord;
>   Clear a straight path for him.
5 >   Every ravine shall be filled in,
>   And every mountain and hill levelled;
>   The corners shall be straightened,
>   And the rough ways made smooth;
6 >   And all mankind shall see God's deliverance."'

7 Crowds of people came out to be baptized by him, and
he said to them: 'You vipers' brood! Who warned you
8 to escape from the coming retribution? Then prove your
repentance by the fruit it bears; and do not begin saying
to yourselves, "We have Abraham for our father." I tell
you that God can make children for Abraham out of
9 these stones here. Already the axe is laid to the roots of
the trees; and every tree that fails to produce good fruit
is cut down and thrown on the fire.'

10,11 The people asked him, 'Then what are we to do?' He
replied, 'The man with two shirts must share with him
who has none, and anyone who has food must do the
12 same.' Among those who came to be baptized were
tax-gatherers, and they said to him, 'Master, what are
13 we to do?' He told them, 'Exact no more than the
14 assessment.' Soldiers on service also asked him, 'And
what of us?' To them he said, 'No bullying; no
blackmail; make do with your pay!'

15 The people were on the tiptoe of expectation, all

wondering about John, whether perhaps he was the Messiah, but he spoke out and said to them all, 'I baptize 16 you with water; but there is one to come who is mightier than I. I am not fit to unfasten his shoes. He will baptize you with the Holy Spirit and with fire. His shovel is 17 ready in his hand, to winnow his threshing-floor and gather the wheat into his granary; but he will burn the chaff on a fire that can never go out.'

In this and many other ways he made his appeal to the 18 people and announced the good news. But Prince Herod, 19 when he was rebuked by him over the affair of his brother's wife Herodias and for his other misdeeds, crowned them all by shutting John up in prison.   20

✻ All four Gospels associate, one way or another, the beginning of the ministry of Jesus with John the Baptist. In Mark, the Baptist appears dressed as a new kind of Elijah who urgently summons Israel to repentance. In Matthew, he also looks like Elijah and knows who Jesus is: 'Do you come to me?...I need rather to be baptized by you' (Matt. 3: 14). In Luke, the coming of John the Baptist is an historic moment; the elaborate dating in 3: 1–2 impresses upon the reader the importance of this renewal of prophecy. Luke presents the Baptist as the last of the prophets before the Messiah. In John's Gospel the Baptist is more self-consciously aware of the significance of Jesus: 'There is the Lamb of God' (John 1: 29, 36).

We can thus detect a tendency as time goes on to make the relationship between Jesus and the Baptist clearer. This is, however, not a case of reading back into the tradition something that had no historical basis. There is good evidence that Jesus himself attached special importance to the Baptist. For Jesus, the Baptist was the last of the prophets of old Israel ('until John, it was the Law and the prophets', Luke 16: 16) and he regarded rejection of John's movement as rejection of God's purpose (Luke 7: 30). Jesus took the coming of John the Baptist as a 'sign' from the Father that the kingdom of God was about to appear.

1. If by *the fifteenth year of the Emperor Tiberius* Luke means fifteen years from the time when Tiberius succeeded Augustus (A.D. 14) this would make the date A.D. 29. If, however, Luke is calculating from the time when Tiberius became joint Emperor with Augustus (A.D. 11–12) the date would be A.D. 26–7.

2. The use of the Old Testament phrase *the word of God came* suggests at once that Luke intends to present John the Baptist predominantly as a prophet, and not so much as 'the Elijah to come' which was the aim of Mark and Matthew. Notice that in Luke John does not appear in the costume of Elijah which he wears in the other two Gospels.

3. Making up one's mind what the baptism given by John meant was a serious business, as Jesus himself indicated later when he asked: 'tell me, was the baptism of John from God or from men?' (Luke 20: 4). John's baptizing was more than just another ritual purificatory act. It was a sign, for those ready to repent, that God was about to act decisively in Israel.

4–6. The passage in Isa. 40: 4 ff. was, to judge from the way it is used in all four Gospels, a text closely associated with the coming messianic age. Luke gives more extensive quotation than any of the other evangelists; no doubt the repetitive use of 'every' and 'all' (the one word means both things in Greek) attracted him as a way of again suggesting the universal character of the mission of Christ.

7. In Luke the phrase *You vipers' brood* is used only by John the Baptist. Matthew, on the other hand, at a number of points blurs the distinction between the teaching of John the Baptist and that of Jesus. So, for instance in Matt. 23: 33, Jesus addresses the lawyers and Pharisees as 'You snakes, you vipers' brood'. This would seem to be Matthew's way of sharpening the conflict between Jesus and his opponents.

44

Perhaps for this reason, Matthew says that the proclamation of John the Baptist was also addressed to 'many of the Pharisees and Sadducees' but there is some evidence that the Baptist's converts were drawn from the general public (Mark 11: 27–33 and Luke 7: 7, 29 ff.) and so Luke's introduction here (*Crowds of people*) is more likely to correspond with the facts.

8. It was a constant temptation for Israel to take the fact of being a 'chosen people' (*we have Abraham for our father*) to mean chosen for privilege, power and prosperity, and therefore, in the last resort, to put ultimate trust in one's nationality or race. But because the judgement of God is serious judgement, it is a specially stern experience for a chosen people: 'You only have I known of all the families of the earth: therefore I will visit upon you all your iniquities' (Amos 3: 2). It is God who creates his Israel; Israel is not a self-made people.

10–14. The response to the proclamation of John must be repentance, and here are particular examples of what repentance might entail. Luke, in a way which is to be characteristic of his Gospel as a whole, stresses the obligations of social justice. The Romans imposed taxes on all citizens under their jurisdiction and sold the right to collect them to the highest bidders. These tax-gathering agencies hired collectors who are the 'tax-gatherers' of the Gospels. There was obviously plenty of scope for exploiting people by demanding more tax than the Romans actually required. This injustice must be renounced, says the Baptist, as a preparation for the new order of things.

15. Luke shares John's interest in the identity of John the Baptist and his relation to Christ (see John 1: 19–23).

16–17. John's baptism with water is contrasted with the Messiah's baptism with the Holy Spirit and fire. It is probable that the original contrast in John's preaching was between water and fire baptisms; water baptism being a preparation for the judgement which comes with the Messiah. See Mal. 4: 1 f. for an Old Testament example of the use of fire as a metaphor for judgement. Soon, and particularly in the Lucan tradition, fire came to be associated with the Holy Spirit (Acts 1: 5), and this association is reflected in the text here.

19. Herod by his action of imprisoning John shows that he does not see him as a 'sign'. Jesus said that to refuse John's baptism amounted to a rejection of God's purpose (Luke 7: 30); to dismiss John made it all the more likely that he, Jesus, would be dismissed as well (Luke 20: 4 ff.). *

THE BAPTISM AND TEMPTATION OF JESUS

21 During a general baptism of the people, when Jesus too
22 had been baptized and was praying, heaven opened and the Holy Spirit descended on him in bodily form like a dove; and there came a voice from heaven, 'Thou art my Son, my Beloved; on thee my favour rests.'

23 When Jesus began his work he was about thirty years old, the son, as people thought, of Joseph, son of Heli,
24 son of Matthat, son of Levi, son of Melchi, son of Jannai,
25 son of Joseph, son of Mattathiah, son of Amos, son of
26 Nahum, son of Esli, son of Naggai, son of Maath, son of Mattathiah, son of Semein, son of Josech, son of Joda,
27 son of Johanan, son of Rhesa, son of Zerubbabel, son of
28 Shealtiel, son of Neri, son of Melchi, son of Addi, son of
29 Cosam, son of Elmadam, son of Er, son of Joshua, son of
30 Eliezer, son of Jorim, son of Matthat, son of Levi, son of Symeon, son of Judah, son of Joseph, son of Jonam, son of
31 Eliakim, son of Melea, son of Menna, son of Mattatha,
32 son of Nathan, son of David, son of Jesse, son of Obed,
33 son of Boaz, son of Salmon, son of Nahshon, son of Amminadab, son of Arni, son of Hezron, son of Perez,
34 son of Judah, son of Jacob, son of Isaac, son of Abraham,

son of Terah, son of Nahor, son of Serug, son of Reu, 35
son of Peleg, son of Eber, son of Shelah, son of Cainan, 36
son of Arpachshad, son of Shem, son of Noah, son of
Lamech, son of Methuselah, son of Enoch, son of Jared, 37
son of Mahalaleel, son of Cainan, son of Enosh, son of 38
Seth, son of Adam, son of God.

Full of the Holy Spirit, Jesus returned from the Jordan, **4**
and for forty days was led by the Spirit up and down the 2
wilderness and tempted by the devil.

All that time he had nothing to eat, and at the end of it
he was famished. The devil said to him, 'If you are the Son 3
of God, tell this stone to become bread.' Jesus answered, 4
'Scripture says, "Man cannot live on bread alone."'

Next the devil led him up and showed him in a flash all 5
the kingdoms of the world. 'All this dominion will I 6
give to you,' he said, 'and the glory that goes with it;
for it has been put in my hands and I can give it to anyone
I choose. You have only to do homage to me and it shall 7
all be yours.' Jesus answered him, 'Scripture says, "You 8
shall do homage to the Lord your God and worship him
alone."'

The devil took him to Jerusalem and set him on the 9
parapet of the temple. 'If you are the Son of God,' he
said, 'throw yourself down; for Scripture says, "He will 10
give his angels orders to take care of you", and again, 11
"They will support you in their arms for fear you should
strike your foot against a stone."' Jesus answered him, 12
'It has been said, "You are not to test the Lord your
God."'

So, having come to the end of all his temptations, the 13
devil departed, biding his time.

✳ The accounts of the baptism and temptation of Jesus are of crucial importance for an understanding of what he believed about himself and about the task committed to him. These narratives are either legends which grew up in the early Church or substantially they go back to Jesus himself. Perhaps he referred to these experiences when talking to his disciples, for example in the later part of the ministry after Caesarea Philippi. There is every reason to think this is so. If we wish to test the possibility that these stories grew up entirely in church tradition we can put them alongside a passage like Matt. 3: 14–15, which looks as if it is some early Christian attempt to get over the difficulty that Jesus accepted a baptism which was 'for the forgiveness of sins', or alongside accounts of the baptism of Jesus in apocryphal Gospels like The Gospel according to the Hebrews or The Gospel of the Ebionites.

21-2. If the account comes ultimately from Jesus himself then a study of the imagery used may provide some indication of the way he experienced this incident. Jesus was a poet and had a poet's perception. During prayer after baptism (Luke marks off the significant moments in the ministry of Jesus by reference to prayer) Jesus saw the *heaven opened*, the Holy Spirit descending *like a dove*, and a voice addressed him personally: '*Thou art my Son*'.

The picture of the *heaven opened* suggests a number of Old Testament passages where God's dramatic coming down on Mount Sinai to give Israel his Law is spoken of in similar language:

Oh that thou wouldest rend the heavens, that thou wouldest come down (Isa. 64: 1);

Bow thy heavens, O Lord, and come down:
Touch the mountains, and they shall smoke (Ps. 144: 5).

The picture of the dove may be an allusion to the spirit of God hovering over the deep in the Genesis account of the creation. It may also be connected with a rabbinic tradition which pictured Israel as a gentle, faithful and submissive dove.

The words of the voice suggest that this event was a final and complete realization by Jesus that God was father to him in a uniquely intimate way, a relationship which, Luke suggests, Jesus was conscious of from an early date (2: 49). Sonship would suggest to Jesus, with his knowledge of the Old Testament, the call of Israel. In the Old Testament Israel is frequently spoken of as the 'son' of God. In Ps. 2, which the first words of the voice seem to echo ('The Lord said unto me, Thou art my son' Ps. 2: 7), the king of Israel is addressed by God as 'my son'. Perhaps, then, after the baptism there came to Jesus this picture of a king summoned to receive from God lordship over the nations. The later words of the voice according to one reading are reminiscent of the opening of the first of the 'servant songs' (Isa. 42: 1) and other passages in Isaiah where the prophet pictures Israel as a 'servant' called by God to a special task which involves humiliation and suffering but ends in triumph. It looks as if Jesus also saw, merging into the picture of the king, the servant who is called by God to a mission of obedience, humility and martyrdom. The other reading given in some manuscripts: 'My Son art thou; this day I have begotten thee' probably results from some copyist wanting to bring the words of the voice into exact accord with verse 7 of Ps. 2.

The four images which can be traced in the account of the baptism, the opening of the heavens, the dove, the king and the servant all suggest that Jesus experienced a unique summons to perform Israel's duty of walking in the way of the Lord.

23–38. In Luke the family-tree of Jesus follows his account of the baptism and is not, as in Matthew, a preface to the whole book and the accounts of the nativity. This may be to reinforce in a different way the points just made. Jesus is Son of David, a true heir to the kingship of Israel; but Luke takes the genealogy back to Adam (in Matthew it goes back only to Abraham) which suggests that he would have us see in

Jesus, as Paul did, the new Adam who in his own life will rewrite the human story.

4: 1–2. Luke here, as elsewhere (cf. 4: 14, 18, 21), apparently wishes to emphasize not only that Jesus was acted upon by the Spirit (Matthew and Mark also say that) but also that he fully possessed the Spirit.

2–13. Again there is no good reason for doubting that the source of this narrative of the temptation was ultimately Jesus himself. It is closely related to a question which other evidence in the Gospels suggests was always in Jesus' mind: what should be the method of his mission? And it is likely that we have here basically Jesus' own picture of the experience which later on he described to his disciples. The order of the temptations varies in Matthew and Luke. In Matthew it is (1) stones, (2) temple, (3) kingdoms; in Luke (1) stones, (2) kingdoms, (3) temple. Matthew probably gives the original sequence. Luke may well have changed this order because he wished to make a general comment about the temptations (Luke 4: 13) and it suited this purpose to end the account with the reply *You are not to test the Lord your God.*

The replies of Jesus all come from that section of the book of Deuteronomy (chs. 6–8) which is concerned with God's summons to Israel and Israel's temptation to disregard it. Presumably Jesus saw himself again going through the temptation of Israel. He was tempted, first, to doubt the reality of the vocation to sonship which he had accepted after the baptism, and to ask also for some satisfying proof from the Father. In acute hunger, and perhaps with Deuteronomy's delectable picture of the plenty of the promised land in mind (Deut. 8: 1–10), Jesus was tempted to anticipate, for his own satisfaction, the bounty which the Father would give, but in his own time and way: '*If you are the Son of God, tell this stone to become bread*' (verse 3). But the first of the many trials of Jesus as he sets out to realize the destiny of Israel is overcome; he declines to put the Father to the test.

The second temptation reminds us of the picture Jesus had in mind after the baptism: the king of Ps. 2 summoned to receive a kingdom. Perhaps like Moses on Mount Pisgah (Deut. 34: 1-4) he is given a vision of the promised land as the kingdom of God. But how should Jesus receive this kingdom? Was it something exclusively his to take as and when he would (as the devil suggests), or was it something which the Father would bestow on him at the right moment? With the same section of Deuteronomy still in mind Jesus turns aside the temptation to think in terms of 'my power and the might of my hand' which would amount to going 'after other gods' to serve and worship them (Deut. 8: 17-19). The new Israel in Jesus overcomes idolatry.

Finally, Jesus is faced with Israel's fundamental and continuing temptation, to demand a 'sign from heaven' which would make it unequivocally clear whether the Lord is among us or not (Exod. 17: 7). To cast himself from the temple would be to put the Father to test. Jesus must not proclaim himself but allow the Father to proclaim him in his own time and way.

Luke ends his account of the temptation by suggesting that trial was a continuing feature of the ministry of Jesus. Later on in this Gospel Jesus is to describe the disciples as 'the men who have stood firmly by me in my times of trial' (22: 28). *

In Galilee: Success and Opposition

JESUS IN THE SYNAGOGUE AT NAZARETH

THEN JESUS, armed with the power of the Spirit, 14 returned to Galilee; and reports about him spread through the whole country-side. He taught in their 15 synagogues and all men sang his praises.

51

16   So he came to Nazareth, where he had been brought up, and went to synagogue on the Sabbath day as he regularly
17 did. He stood up to read the lesson and was handed the scroll of the prophet Isaiah. He opened the scroll and found the passage which says,

18 'The spirit of the Lord is upon me because he has anointed me;
    He has sent me to announce good news to the poor,
    To proclaim release for prisoners and recovery of sight for the blind;
    To let the broken victims go free,
19 To proclaim the year of the Lord's favour.'

20 He rolled up the scroll, gave it back to the attendant, and sat down; and all eyes in the synagogue were fixed on him.
21   He began to speak: 'Today', he said, 'in your very
22 hearing this text has come true.' There was a general stir of admiration; they were surprised that words of such grace should fall from his lips. 'Is not this Joseph's son?'
23 they asked. Then Jesus said, 'No doubt you will quote the proverb to me, "Physician, heal yourself!", and say, "We have heard of all your doings at Capernaum; do the
24 same here in your own home town." I tell you this,' he went on: 'no prophet is recognized in his own country.
25 There were many widows in Israel, you may be sure, in Elijah's time, when for three years and six months the skies never opened, and famine lay hard over the whole
26 country; yet it was to none of those that Elijah was sent, but to a widow at Sarepta in the territory of Sidon.
27 Again, in the time of the prophet Elisha there were many lepers in Israel, and not one of them was healed, but only

Naaman, the Syrian.' At these words the whole congre- 28
gation were infuriated. They leapt up, threw him out of 29
the town, and took him to the brow of the hill on which
it was built, meaning to hurl him over the edge. But he 30
walked straight through them all, and went away.

✻ Like John, Luke is willing to rearrange the order of events
to emphasize a point. Both Matthew and Mark place this
incident later on in the Galilean ministry of Jesus, and Luke
himself, at 4: 23, suggests that other things had been happening before this. Luke puts it at the head of his account of the
mission of Jesus so as to illustrate the theme which John
described as Jesus entering 'his own realm' and being rejected
(John 1: 11). Jesus turned first to the Israel of his day. When
Israel as a whole rejected him, he saw himself as the corner-
stone of a new Israel (Luke 20: 17) and those who did
respond to him entered it. The text and the address suggest a
miniature outline of the actual course of the mission of Jesus,
and it is interesting to compare it with the speech and attitude
of Stephen in Acts 6: 10 — 7: 60. The parallelism is deliberate;
for Luke, the basic pattern of the life and work of a disciple of
Jesus was bound to turn out very like that of the master.

14. In Matthew (4: 12) and Mark (1: 14) the beginning of
the mission of Jesus coincides with the end of John the Baptist's.
Luke, on the other hand, seems to have preferred to associate
the main turning-points in the life of Jesus with the working
of the Holy Spirit rather than the career of John the Baptist.
In Acts the missions of the Christian apostles are similarly
'punctuated' with references to the action of the Holy Spirit.
Read in conjunction with Acts it would seem that the
evangelist saw this episode as a pointer to the mission to the
Gentiles which would come after the outpouring of the
Spirit at Pentecost (Acts 2: 1–4).

16. Like his followers in Acts, Jesus used to attend synagogue on the Sabbath. This passage gives us some idea of
Jewish worship at the time of Jesus. Jesus reads a lesson from

the prophets; previous readings were from the Law (Genesis–Deuteronomy). Perhaps the order of lessons from the Law and the prophets had been fixed in a lectionary, in which case the passage read was not Jesus' own choice. Jesus must have accepted the invitation to read, which the president of the synagogue used to extend to a visiting rabbi.

21. Jesus' characteristic method was not to proclaim himself in so many words, but to summon his hearers to see what was happening in their time, the words being said and the deeds done, as pointers to the presence of God's kingdom. The text (Isa. 61: 1–2) and Jesus' comment on it show that he expected his listeners to recognize the presence of Isaiah's prophet-servant engaged in bringing to fruition God's designs for Israel. The irony is that when the Lord comes into his own, his own can at first see nothing but one of themselves! *Is not this Joseph's son?* (verse 22). And at the end they wish to throw him out as an alien (verse 29).

22–3. The crowd are surprised that one who seems to be just one of themselves (*Is not this Joseph's son?*) should suggest that Old Testament history has been leading up to him. Jesus' reply shows that he is aware of the temptation to give some visible indisputable proof of his claim.

24–7. The Old Testament episodes referred to here are recorded in 1 Kings 17–18 and 2 Kings 5. These references of Jesus suggest that Israel by demanding first her own kind of satisfying proofs ('*do the same here in your own home town*') will miss the Messiah, while more receptive outsiders will be able to recognize him.

28–30. We have suggested above that the whole section Luke 4: 14–30 is a kind of prologue to the record of the activity of Jesus. These verses may therefore have been so worded as to suggest the end of his ministry, when a crowd did take him outside a town and kill him. It is not likely that such a violent reaction to Jesus took place right at the beginning of his ministry. Luke's account of the reaction of the crowd to the speech of Stephen when 'they made one rush at

him and, flinging him out of the city, set about stoning him'
(Acts 7: 58) is meant to remind the reader that Jesus too had
met with similar experiences. ✲

FIRST HEALINGS

Coming down to Capernaum, a town in Galilee, he 31
taught the people on the Sabbath, and they were 32
astounded at his teaching, for what he said had the note
of authority. Now there was a man in the synagogue 33
possessed by a devil, an unclean spirit. He shrieked at the
top of his voice, 'What do you want with us, Jesus of 34
Nazareth? Have you come to destroy us? I know who
you are—the Holy One of God.' Jesus rebuked him: 35
'Be silent', he said, 'and come out of him.' Then the
devil, after throwing the man down in front of the people,
left him without doing him any injury. Amazement fell 36
on them all and they said to one another: 'What is there
in this man's words? He gives orders to the unclean spirits
with authority and power, and out they go.' So the news 37
spread, and he was the talk of the whole district.

On leaving the synagogue he went to Simon's house. 38
Simon's mother-in-law was in the grip of a high fever;
and they asked him to help her. He came and stood 39
over her and rebuked the fever. It left her, and she got up
at once and waited on them.

At sunset all who had friends suffering from one disease 40
or another brought them to him; and he laid his hands
on them one by one and cured them. Devils also came 41
out of many of them, shouting, 'You are the Son of God.'
But he rebuked them and forbade them to speak, because
they knew that he was the Messiah.

42   When day broke he went out and made his way to a lonely spot. But the people went in search of him, and when they came to where he was they pressed him not to
43   leave them. But he said, 'I must give the good news of the kingdom of God to the other towns also, for that is
44   what I was sent to do.' So he proclaimed the Gospel in the synagogues of Judaea.

* Jesus shared the common view of his time that mental derangement was caused by devil-possession. The mentally unbalanced person so often presents a picture of one who has lost control of himself and is being driven relentlessly by some demonic destructive force that it is easy to understand how men came to think in terms of demon-possession. The cure suggested here may have been brought about through Jesus' power to restore fundamental self-confidence in the unbalanced. He points out later that he is not alone in having this power and the question which the action of Jesus suggests is whether he himself is possessed by God or a demon: 'If it is by Beelzebub that I cast out devils, by whom do your own people drive them out?' (Luke 11: 19).

36–7. Whether he is a sign of the presence of the kingdom of God, or of its adversary, is for men to decide.

38–9. Simon's house at Capernaum seems to have been used by Jesus as a kind of headquarters during the early stages of the mission. Jesus is spoken of as rebuking the fever (cf. 4: 35); this suggests that it is regarded by Luke as a form of demon-possession.

41. The irony of the situation is that while men discuss who Jesus is, the devils who are being expelled know! Jesus' healing ends involuntary crying out (right though it may be). He restores the condition for true faith: voluntary response. Faith is a free decision, and involves more than mere verbal labelling.

43. Jesus' mission is not something he makes up for him-

self in his own time and way as he goes along. He *must give the good news of the kingdom of God* because this is a task laid upon him by the Father. The kingdom of God is the mysterious activity of God's sovereignty. It discloses itself in the content and manner of the actions and words of Jesus, further examples of which now follow. *

THE CALL OF SIMON

One day as he stood by the Lake of Gennesaret, and the **5** people crowded upon him to listen to the word of God, he noticed two boats lying at the water's edge; the fisher- 2 men had come ashore and were washing their nets. He 3 got into one of the boats, which belonged to Simon, and asked him to put out a little way from the shore; then he went on teaching the crowds from his seat in the boat. When he had finished speaking, he said to Simon, 'Put 4 out into deep water and let down your nets for a catch.' Simon answered, 'Master, we were hard at work all 5 night and caught nothing at all; but if you say so, I will let down the nets.' They did so and made a big haul of 6 fish; and their nets began to split. So they signalled to 7 their partners in the other boat to come and help them. This they did, and loaded both boats to the point of sinking. When Simon saw what had happened he fell 8 at Jesus's knees and said, 'Go, Lord, leave me, sinner that I am!' For he and all his companions were amazed at 9 the catch they had made; so too were his partners James 10 and John, Zebedee's sons. 'Do not be afraid,' said Jesus to Simon; 'from now on you will be catching men.' As 11 soon as they had brought the boats to land, they left everything and followed him.

* In Luke the call of Simon Peter is given much greater prominence than in Mark or Matthew (see Mark 1: 16–20 and Matt. 4: 18–22). This may well be because, with an eye to the story of Acts, he wishes to bring out the significance of Peter among the disciples as a prelude to his leadership in the early Church.

A similar story, again symbolical of the future mission of Peter and the Church is given in John 21: 1–14 where the risen Christ commissions Peter as the shepherd of the new community. *

HEALING OF A LEPER AND A PARALYTIC

12 He was once in a certain town where there happened to be a man covered with leprosy; seeing Jesus, he bowed to the ground and begged his help. 'Sir,' he said, 'if only you 13 will, you can cleanse me.' Jesus stretched out his hand, touched him, and said, 'Indeed I will; be clean again.' 14 The leprosy left him immediately. Jesus then ordered him not to tell anybody. 'But go,' he said, 'show yourself to the priest, and make the offering laid down by Moses for 15 your cleansing; that will certify the cure.' But the talk about him spread all the more; great crowds gathered to 16 hear him and to be cured of their ailments. And from time to time he would withdraw to lonely places for prayer.

17 One day he was teaching, and Pharisees and teachers of the law were sitting round. People had come from every village of Galilee and from Judaea and Jerusalem, and 18 the power of God was with him to heal the sick. Some men appeared carrying a paralysed man on a bed. They tried to bring him in and set him down in front of Jesus, 19 but finding no way to do so because of the crowd, they went up on to the roof and let him down through the

tiling, bed and all, into the middle of the company in
front of Jesus. When Jesus saw their faith, he said, 'Man, 20
your sins are forgiven you.'

The lawyers and the Pharisees began saying to them- 21
selves, 'Who is this fellow with his blasphemous talk?
Who but God alone can forgive sins?' But Jesus knew 22
their thoughts and answered them: 'Why do you harbour
thoughts like these? Is it easier to say, "Your sins are 23
forgiven you", or to say, "Stand up and walk"? But 24
to convince you that the Son of Man has the right on
earth to forgive sins'—he turned to the paralysed man—
'I say to you, stand up, take your bed, and go home.'
And at once he rose to his feet before their eyes, took up 25
the bed he had been lying on, and went home praising
God. They were all lost in amazement and praised God; 26
filled with awe they said, 'You would never believe the
things we have seen today.'

* 12–16. The healing of lepers was for Jesus one of the signs
of the presence of the messianic age in him, as his reply to
John the Baptist's question shows: 'Go...and tell John what
you have seen and heard: how the blind recover their sight,
the lame walk, the lepers are clean...' (Luke 7: 22).

14. Jesus sends the leper back to the priests who, according
to Lev. 14: 1 ff., were expected to satisfy themselves as to the
cure and to prescribe the sacrifices necessary before the
formerly unclean man could rejoin the community. The
Greek phrase translated *that will certify the cure* (literally in the
Greek 'as a witness to them') might be intended to mean 'as
a sign that a mighty power is in your midst'.

16. One of the frequent references in Luke to Jesus' practice
of prayer. Luke, more than the other synoptic evangelists,
presents Christ as the model for the Christian's life of prayer.

17–26. This is a classic example of Jesus' manner in his ministry, and of his irony. Incidentally, it gives us some idea of his attitude to what we call miracles. Whenever Jesus is asked direct questions about himself or the nature of his mission his habit is to reply in such a way as to bring the speaker to face the question again. Who he is and what he is doing—this is something his questioners must answer for themselves. To do it for them, by identifying himself in so many words, would be to reduce their freedom to choose. His mission is to liberate men, not to exploit them.

Jesus ironically suggests that while it may be easier to say *Your sins are forgiven you* than *Stand up and walk*, since no visible evidence is possible to confirm its truth, the second saying is in a sense the easier to hear since people are more interested in the beneficial results of a cure than the rigours of repentance. Jesus in fact leaves his critics to answer for themselves the question 'Has then the Son of Man the right on earth to forgive sins?' Again, his healing power might be the sign of a demon-possession; in which case they are victims of it also! 'If it is by Beelzebub that I cast out devils, by whom do your own people drive them out?' (Luke 11: 19).

24. The *Son of Man* is an enigmatic term deliberately chosen by Jesus (it is found only in the Gospels and once in Acts 7: 56) as a way of pointing to the meaning of his mission. A number of backgrounds to the term have been suggested, two of which are important:

(*a*) In Dan. 7 after the procession of the beasts representing political power there appears (verse 13) 'one like unto a son of man' and he is invested with kingship by God, 'the ancient of days'. Later in the chapter (verse 22) this 'son of man' is apparently identical with the people of Israel, the 'saints of the Most High' who have suffered and then been crowned with glory.

(*b*) In the book of Ezekiel the prophet is again and again addressed as the 'son of man'. This book had a great influence on Jesus (see, for instance, chapter 34 on the shepherd and the flock, and compare the use of this metaphor in the teaching of Jesus, both in the Synoptic Gospels and John, and also the summons of Ezekiel to be 'a sign' (12: 6, 11; 24: 24)). It may well be that Jesus was attracted to the prophet's use of this term for one who might seem to others weak, powerless, a figure of humiliation, but who was through the Spirit one who nevertheless carries out the will of God.

Jesus uses the term in an objective third-personal kind of way and speaks of the Son of Man as one who both comes in humiliation and suffering and also in glory and triumph. Who this figure is and when these things shall be is for men to recognize. In view of the closeness between his presentation of the 'way' of the Son of Man and the 'way' of the disciples Jesus may also have thought at times of the 'Son of Man' as Israel, the people of God, now being reconstructed by his mission, through the action of the Spirit in accordance with the will of the Father. This 'Son of Man' as used by Jesus sometimes refers to an individual, sometimes to a community, sometimes to both. He is like Daniel's 'son of man': a figure of suffering who will yet be given a kingdom. The implication is that a community (Israel) is personified by an individual (Jesus). *

THE PRESENCE OF THE BRIDEGROOM OF ISRAEL

Later, when he went out, he saw a tax-gatherer, Levi by 27 name, at his seat in the custom-house. He said to him, 'Follow me'; and he rose to his feet, left everything 28 behind, and followed him.

Afterwards Levi held a big reception in his house for 29 Jesus; among the guests was a large party of tax-gatherers and others. The Pharisees and the lawyers of their sect 30 complained to his disciples: 'Why do you eat and drink', they said, 'with tax-gatherers and sinners?' Jesus 31

answered them: 'It is not the healthy that need a doctor,
32 but the sick; I have not come to invite virtuous people,
but to call sinners to repentance.'

33   Then they said to him, 'John's disciples are much given
to fasting and the practice of prayer, and so are the
34 disciples of the Pharisees; but yours eat and drink.' Jesus
replied, 'Can you make the bridegroom's friends fast
35 while the bridegroom is with them? But a time will
come: the bridegroom will be taken away from them,
and that will be the time for them to fast.'

36   He told them this parable also: 'No one tears a piece
from a new cloak to patch an old one; if he does, he will
have made a hole in the new cloak, and the patch from
37 the new will not match the old. Nor does anyone put
new wine into old wine-skins; if he does, the new wine
will burst the skins, the wine will be wasted, and the skins
38,39 ruined. Fresh skins for new wine! And no one after
drinking old wine wants new; for he says, "The old wine
is good."'

☆ 27–8. In Mark and Luke this disciple is called Levi. In
Matthew (9: 9) his name is given as Matthew. The same person
is meant since Mark (3: 18) has Matthew in his list of the
twelve. Possibly the man had the two names, Matthew and
Levi.

    29–32. Another good example of the ironical manner of
Jesus. His hearers are left free to regard themselves as *virtuous*
if that is their wish! But the irony of Jesus is such that even
if it embarrasses, it leaves the way open for remedial action:
repentance.

    33–9. It seems to have been easy to classify John the Baptist
and his disciples as ascetics, but not so easy to make out where
Jesus and his followers stood. Jesus by his reply suggests that

the question that ought to be asked is whether the bridegroom of Israel and his attendants are present or not. If you can answer that, implies Jesus, the question of fasting will answer itself. The incognito appearance of Jesus as the bridegroom of Israel is the point of John's story of the turning of water into wine at Cana-in-Galilee (John 2: 1–11). This may well have been influenced by this section in Luke since it contains the same two themes of the mysterious hidden bridegroom and the new and old wines. God's role as the bridegroom of Israel is spoken of, for example, in Hosea: '...I will betroth thee unto me for ever' (2: 19), or Isa. 54: 5: 'thy Maker is thine husband; the Lord of hosts is his name'. Jesus sees his mission as Israel's wedding festival, and therefore it is no time for fasting.

39. This saying might have referred to those (whether John the Baptist's disciples or Israel in general) who prefer the conservatism of the old order, and lack the enterprise to accept the new. This conservative caution, Jesus indicates, again and again hinders a man from seeing the new and critical character of things taking place in front of his eyes. An example is in the incident which follows. ✷

BREAKING THE SABBATH

One Sabbath he was going through the cornfields, and **6** his disciples were plucking the ears of corn, rubbing them in their hands, and eating them. Some of the Pharisees 2 said, 'Why are you doing what is forbidden on the Sabbath?' Jesus answered, 'So you have not read what 3 David did when he and his men were hungry? He went 4 into the House of God and took the consecrated loaves to eat and gave them to his men, though priests alone are allowed to eat them, and no one else.' He also said, 'The 5 Son of Man is sovereign even over the Sabbath.'

6   On another Sabbath he had gone to synagogue and was
teaching. There happened to be a man in the congrega-
7 tion whose right arm was withered; and the lawyers and
Pharisees were on the watch to see whether Jesus would
cure him on the Sabbath, so that they could find a charge
8 to bring against him. But he knew what was in their
minds and said to the man with the withered arm, 'Get
up and stand out here.' So he got up and stood there.
9 Then Jesus said to them, 'I put the question to you: is it
permitted to do good or to do evil on the Sabbath, to
10 save life or to destroy it?' He looked round at them all
and then said to the man, 'Stretch out your arm.' He
11 did so, and his arm was restored. But they were beside
themselves with anger, and began to discuss among
themselves what they could do to Jesus.

✷ Many of the actions of Jesus are associated with the
Sabbath; and this is not likely to have been due simply to
accident. More probably Jesus deliberately chose the Sabbath
as the setting of his 'mighty works'. Already in Judaism
before Christ the Sabbath had come to be a symbol of the
peace, restoration and well-being of Israel and was to be one
of the signs that the messianic age had come (Isa. 14: 3). Jesus
indicates by his actions that, for those ready to respond, here
in his mission are the marks of the promised Sabbath of Israel.

2. The Law (Exod. 20: 10) forbade work on the Sabbath,
and Jewish interpretation had analysed in very great detail
exactly what constituted 'work'. 'Reaping' was included in
the list, and this is what the Pharisees are referring to here.

3. Jesus refers to the incident related in 1 Sam. 21: 1–6.
He implies that if David could set aside prescriptions of the
Law the fact that he, Jesus, is now doing the same thing could
mean that his hearers have to do with a new and greater
David. If this interpretation is right, here is another example

of the indirect, oblique, manner of Jesus in signifying the meaning of his ministry. There is another form of this in the next episode.

5. Again this answer implies that in Jesus and his disciples something of new and decisive importance is taking place. The Pharisees, he implies, are being confronted with a new order of things which is more important than the Law itself.

7. The rabbis ruled that where life was in danger it was permissible to treat the sick on the Sabbath. This case of paralysis would not count as a danger to life, and so the Pharisees wait to see if Jesus will commit an offence by healing the man.

9. Again an example of the ironical manner of Jesus. The Pharisees' answer to Jesus' question would be 'to do good, of course'. Yet they were using the Sabbath to prepare means of bringing about his destruction! *

CHOOSING THE TWELVE

During this time he went out one day into the hills to 12 pray, and spent the night in prayer to God. When day 13 broke he called his disciples to him, and from among them he chose twelve and named them Apostles: Simon, 14 to whom he gave the name of Peter, and Andrew his brother, James and John, Philip and Bartholomew, Matthew and Thomas, James son of Alphaeus, and 15 Simon who was called the Zealot, Judas son of James, and 16 Judas Iscariot who turned traitor.

He came down the hill with them and took his stand 17 on level ground. There was a large concourse of his disciples and great numbers of people from Jerusalem and Judaea and from the seaboard of Tyre and Sidon, who had come to listen to him, and to be cured of their diseases. Those who were troubled with unclean spirits were cured; 18

19 and everyone in the crowd was trying to touch him, because power went out from him and cured them all.

✴ Luke marks another turning point in the ministry of Jesus by a reference to prayer, and this time all-night prayer. The choosing of a group of twelve suggests that Jesus may have seen himself and the Twelve as called to enact God's establishment of the kingdom through his Messiah and the twelve attendants of the new Israel. In them people could see a dramatization of the Old Testament picture of God bringing the twelve tribes of Israel to the promised land. This is how he pictures the kingdom in its final glory: they will 'sit on thrones as judges of the twelve tribes of Israel' (Luke 22: 30). He and the Twelve are signs of the presence of the kingdom to the eyes of faith.

13. Apostle is a word used so frequently in the writings of Luke, both Gospel and Acts, and was used so seldom in the other Gospels, that we may safely assume that apostleship is a major theme in Luke's mind. Jesus was himself *the* Apostle, the 'sent one' (see Luke 4: 43) and he sends out his church into the world through the work of apostles.

17. Perhaps with the Old Testament treatment of Mount Sinai in mind, Luke finds a special significance in the mountain. It is above all else the place of God's revelation where God meets those specially near to him. Jesus now turns to go down the slopes to address the people below in a way that reminds one of Moses going down Mount Sinai to give God's Law to Israel (see Exod. 19). ✴

BEATITUDES AND WOES

20 Then turning to his disciples he began to speak:

'How blest are you who are poor; the kingdom of God is yours.

21 'How blest are you who now go hungry; your hunger shall be satisfied.

'How blest are you who weep now; you shall laugh.

'How blest you are when men hate you, when they 22 outlaw you and insult you, and ban your very name as infamous, because of the Son of Man. On that day be 23 glad and dance for joy; for assuredly you have a rich reward in heaven; in just the same way did their fathers treat the prophets.

'But alas for you who are rich; you have had your 24 time of happiness.

'Alas for you who are well-fed now; you shall go 25 hungry.

'Alas for you who laugh now; you shall mourn and weep.

'Alas for you when all speak well of you; just so did 26 their fathers treat the false prophets.

✳ In Luke the first extended summary of Jesus' teaching is explicitly directed to disciples. What now follows is a description of the life of the follower of Jesus. It begins with Luke's version of the beatitudes; these differ in number, wording and style of address from the version which appears in Matt. 5: 3–10.

20. The 'sermon on the plain' begins, like the sermon in the synagogue (4: 18) with a reference to 'the poor'. The use of this term by Jesus has an Old Testament background. Those who were left behind in Jerusalem after its capture in 586 B.C. were in a destitute state, and they became a symbol of poor and defenceless people who yet remain loyal to God, as in Ps. 72: 2:

> He shall judge thy people with righteousness,
> And thy poor with judgement.

Jesus uses the word in this sense here, and necessarily there is the implication that in the body of his disciples can be seen the shape of the new Israel.

21. The blessing of Christ falls on those whose compassion gives them an acute sense of the tragedy of life. Looking at the Gospel as a whole Luke seems to suggest that there are two kinds of weeping: weeping before men and weeping before God. Weeping before men can become a sentimental indulgence and in Luke the weeping of the daughters of Jerusalem is shown to be of that kind (Luke 23: 27–8). But there is a weeping before God which springs not from sentimentalism but from repentance.

22. Jesus saw that his mission, as the way of the Son of Man, was in the tradition of the Old Testament prophets, and therefore likely to meet with the same kind of hostile reaction. There is again irony in the way Jesus uses the idea of reward in his teaching. There *is* reward, he teaches; men can be confident of that, but the reward is of such a kind that it can only come to those who have learnt not to want a reward! So here. His true followers will be entirely devoted to walking in his way and they will have the reward that can only be received by those who have ceased to think of themselves. The reward is not of their seeking.

24. In Luke, Jesus condemns riches outright. Zacchaeus is saved, rich though he is, but we are told that he gave half his possessions to charity (Luke 19: 8). Jesus warns that the possession of riches is very hazardous and makes discipleship specially difficult. In Luke there is a tendency to extend this element in the teaching of Jesus in a number of episodes and sayings (the parables of the rich fool (12: 13–21) and 'Dives' and Lazarus (16: 29–31)).

Some have doubted whether these 'woes' are genuine words of Jesus, partly because they are found nowhere else in the Gospels, and partly because they seem to contradict the teaching about love to one's enemies which follows immediately in Luke's Gospel. But it is obvious that Luke did not feel any contradiction and it is more likely, as the new translation brings out, that Jesus is lamenting complacency and the attitude of not caring which, he implies, are more

than likely to result from wealth, comfort, good fortune and
fame. ✻

ON LOVE

'But to you who hear me I say: 27

'Love your enemies; do good to those who hate you;
bless those who curse you; pray for those who treat you 28
spitefully. When a man hits you on the cheek, offer him 29
the other cheek too; when a man takes your coat, let
him have your shirt as well. Give to everyone who asks 30
you; when a man takes what is yours, do not demand it
back. Treat others as you would like them to treat you. 31
    'If you love only those who love you, what credit is 32
that to you? Even sinners love those who love them.
Again, if you do good only to those who do good to you, 33
what credit is that to you? Even sinners do as much.
And if you lend only where you expect to be repaid, 34
what credit is that to you? Even sinners lend to each
other if they are to be repaid in full. But you must love 35
your enemies and do good; and lend without expecting
any return; and you will have a rich reward: you will
be sons of the Most High, because he himself is kind to
the ungrateful and wicked. Be compassionate as your 36
Father is compassionate.
    'Pass no judgement, and you will not be judged; do 37
not condemn, and you will not be condemned; acquit,
and you will be acquitted; give, and gifts will be given 38
you. Good measure, pressed down, shaken together, and
running over, will be poured into your lap; for whatever
measure you deal out to others will be dealt to you in
return.'

✻ Jesus' teaching on love, as given in Luke, points, more than Matthew's version (Matt. 5: 39 ff.), to Jesus himself as the model of his own teaching. This comes out in Luke's treatment of the passion where Jesus is an embodiment of his teaching in this passage that a man should pray for those who treat him spitefully (23: 34). The Christian who acts in this way will be pointing to his master, Christ. An example of this is Stephen who prays for those who were stoning him: 'Lord, do not hold this sin against them' (Acts 7: 60).

29. Jesus has two pictures in mind: an act of physical violence and a robbery. These pictures are not to be taken literally; what Christians must do as disciples is not laid down by Jesus in detail beforehand. But when all has been said, such sayings, insisting, as Plato did, that it is better to suffer an injustice than to do one, are difficult to obey. They remain, however, the goal towards which the Christian ethical ideal must be directed.

30. Again a hard saying. It may be true that if applied literally it could be a bad thing for the individual and chaotic for society; nevertheless the saying implies that, in spite of the risks, it is better to err on the side of generosity.

35. The motive for the love of enemies and a generous attitude is to be the imitation of God, who loves in an unconditional way. The manuscripts vary a little here. Some have: 'lend without ever giving up hope'; others read: 'lend without giving up hope of anyone'. The differences seem to have arisen from reading the first half of this verse as one clause meaning 'Do all this and do not give up anyone as hopeless', or from reading the clause about loans as a separate entity, meaning 'Do not lend with an eye on getting it back'.

37. As they stand, these words sound as if Jesus was condemning the practice of law as such, but elsewhere he assumes the continuing existence and necessity for lawcourts (Luke 12: 57–9). Rather the saying is a warning against trying to take God's judgement into our own hands. Ultimate judgement is something that only God can give, and our judge-

ments, at best, are so partial, based as they are on imperfect knowledge, that it is better to judge oneself than others.

38. Generosity of love to others will be more than matched by the boundless favour of God—a reward incomparably richer than we can imagine. ✳

SAYINGS ON DISCIPLESHIP

He also offered them a parable: 'Can one blind man be 39 guide to another? Will they not both fall into the ditch? A pupil is not superior to his teacher; but everyone, when 40 his training is complete, will reach his teacher's level.

'Why do you look at the speck of sawdust in your 41 brother's eye, with never a thought for the great plank in your own? How can you say to your brother, "My 42 dear brother, let me take the speck out of your eye", when you are blind to the plank in your own? You hypocrite! First take the plank out of your own eye, and then you will see clearly to take the speck out of your brother's.

'There is no such thing as a good tree producing worth- 43 less fruit, nor yet a worthless tree producing good fruit. For each tree is known by its own fruit: you do not 44 gather figs from thistles, and you do not pick grapes from brambles. A good man produces good from the store of 45 good within himself; and an evil man from evil within produces evil. For the words that the mouth utters come from the overflowing of the heart.

'Why do you keep calling me "Lord, Lord"—and 46 never do what I tell you? Everyone who comes to me 47 and hears what I say, and acts upon it—I will show you what he is like. He is like a man who, in building his 48 house, dug deep and laid the foundations on rock.

When the flood came, the river burst upon that house, but could not shift it, because it had been soundly built.
49 But he who hears and does not act is like a man who built his house on the soil without foundations. As soon as the river burst upon it, the house collapsed, and fell with a great crash.'

* 39–42. These parables show how Jesus saw the relationship between disciples and himself.

39. Discipleship means following someone who knows the way; as a result one becomes like the guide. These sayings remind one of John's presentation of Jesus as the way, or the descriptions of Jesus in the Letter to Hebrews as the 'new, living way' (Heb. 10: 20).

By following Jesus the disciples are implying that he is no blind guide but knows the way.

40. It is the destiny of the disciple to become like his master.

41–2. Insight into the reliability of others grows proportionately with genuine self-observation.

43–5. In this saying, again, Jesus seems to have discipleship and its relation to himself in mind. How is the disciple to tell whether the mission of Jesus is worth giving up one's life for? This is a frequent theme in Luke: 'Are you the one who is to come, or are we to expect some other?' (7: 20). The criterion for Jesus is whether bad things are continually and consistently likely to come from good sources, like rotten fruit from a good tree. That is a judgement which disciples must make for themselves.

46–9. Again these sayings look as if they may have been parables on the theme of lordship and discipleship. Like Jesus who built his house (the Church) on a firm foundation, the 'rock' of Peter, the disciple must build his house on the rock which Jesus himself is. This is what calling Jesus 'Lord' means; the kind of readiness to accept what he says which is about to be illustrated in a Gentile, the Roman centurion. *

THE CENTURION'S SERVANT AND THE
WIDOW'S SON AT NAIN

When he had finished addressing the people, he went to 7
Capernaum. A centurion there had a servant whom he 2
valued highly; this servant was ill and near to death.
Hearing about Jesus, he sent some Jewish elders with 3
the request that he would come and save his servant's
life. They approached Jesus and pressed their petition 4
earnestly: 'He deserves this favour from you,' they said,
'for he is a friend of our nation and it is he who built us 5
our synagogue.' Jesus went with them; but when he was 6
not far from the house, the centurion sent friends with
this message: 'Do not trouble further, sir; it is not for
me to have you under my roof, and that is why I did not 7
presume to approach you in person. But say the word
and my servant will be cured. I know, for in my position 8
I am myself under orders, with soldiers under me. I say
to one, "Go", and he goes; to another, "Come here",
and he comes; and to my servant, "Do this", and he does
it.' When Jesus heard this, he admired the man, and, 9
turning to the crowd that was following him, he said,
'I tell you, nowhere, even in Israel, have I found faith
like this.' And the messengers returned to the house and 10
found the servant in good health.

Afterwards Jesus went to a town called Nain, accom- 11
panied by his disciples and a large crowd. As he 12
approached the gate of the town he met a funeral. The
dead man was the only son of his widowed mother; and
many of the townspeople were there with her. When 13
the Lord saw her his heart went out to her, and he said,

14 'Weep no more.' With that he stepped forward and laid his hand on the bier; and the bearers halted. Then he
15 spoke: 'Young man, rise up!' The dead man sat up and began to talk; and Jesus gave him back to his mother.
16 Deep awe fell upon them all, and they praised God. 'A great prophet has arisen among us', they said, and
17 again, 'God has shown his care for his people.' The story of what he had done ran through all parts of Judaea and the whole neighbourhood.

✳ There now begins a section on the meaning of John the Baptist's mission and its relation to Jesus. In placing the episodes of the centurion's servant and the widow's son at Nain at the head of this section Luke may have been thinking of Jesus' reply to John the Baptist's question (Luke 7: 18–23). This reply includes healing and the raising of the dead (7: 22) as signs which ought to indicate who Jesus is. It is a further pointer to the readiness of non-Jews to accept Jesus, which is to be one of the main themes of Acts.

1–10. Luke sees the incident of the healing of the Roman centurion's servant as a miniature representation of the coming of the Gentiles to Christ. Luke would have had this at the back of his mind as the subject of his second volume, Acts. The approach of the centurion to Jesus from a distance through Jewish intermediaries suggests the conversion of the Gentile world through the new Israel which Jesus is forming.

11–17. Raising from the dead is the most difficult of the miraculous actions of Jesus for the modern man to accept. We need first to look at the kind of tradition in the New Testament that he did so. There are three occasions on which Jesus is reported to have brought back to life people who had died: Jairus' daughter, the widow's son at Nain, and (in John) the raising of Lazarus. It is possible to trace a development of dramatic content in these narratives. In Mark and Luke Jairus' daughter is said to be seriously ill, and later a message comes to say that she is dead. In Matthew the story begins with the announcement that she has just died. Here in the episode of the widow's son at Nain the man is not only dead but his funeral is taking place. In John it is even more decisive: Lazarus 'had already been four days in the tomb' (John 11: 17). We cannot know for certain what historical events lie behind the record of these incidents. Leaving aside John's treatment of the Lazarus story, which cannot be understood apart from a study of John's purpose in the Fourth Gospel as a whole, it could be that behind the stories of Jairus' daughter and the widow's son at Nain were originally cases of healing, and that in the transmission of the material the cures have been dramatized into raisings.

Another possible influence on Luke's account of the widow's son at Nain is that of the Old Testament stories of raisings from the dead. When we recall that it is characteristic of Luke to treat Jesus as a new Elijah, it is not surprising to find that the account of Elijah's raising the only son of a widow from the dead in 1 Kings 17: 17–24 seems to have influenced the way the evangelist has recounted this incident. In fact Luke may well have seen it as an amplification of Jesus' reference in his synagogue sermon at Nazareth (4: 26) to Elijah's visit to the widow. The phrase that Jesus *gave him back to his mother* echoes an identical phrase in 1 Kings 17: 23 and the parallelism seems to be deliberate from the way the crowd shout out '*A great prophet has arisen among us*' (like Elijah). Again, if the mind at work behind this Gospel was akin to that of the writer of John's Gospel the reader may be intended to take this miracle as foreshadowing the death of Christ (*the* only Son). Similarly in John the raising of Lazarus is meant to point forward to him who is the resurrection and the life. The Greek word used for 'only son' is the same in Luke and John. If there is allegory in this story, it links up with certain tendencies in John's Gospel. The figure of the weeping mother in this story may be intended to suggest Mother Israel. Jesus is the one who restores to her her lost children.

For the figure of Israel as a mother weeping for her lost ones see Jer. 31: 15 (Rachel) and 2 Esdras 9: 38 — 10: 4 (Mother Zion). ✳

THE SIGNIFICANCE OF JOHN THE BAPTIST

18 John too was informed of all this by his disciples.
19 Summoning two of their number he sent them to the Lord with this message: 'Are you the one who is to
20 come, or are we to expect some other?' The messengers made their way to Jesus and said, 'John the Baptist has sent us to you: he asks, "Are you the one who is to come,
21 or are we to expect some other?"' There and then he cured many sufferers from diseases, plagues, and evil spirits; and on many blind people he bestowed sight.
22 Then he gave them his answer: 'Go', he said, 'and tell John what you have seen and heard: how the blind recover their sight, the lame walk, the lepers are clean, the deaf hear, the dead are raised to life, the poor are
23 hearing the good news—and happy is the man who does not find me a stumbling-block.'

24 After John's messengers had left, Jesus began to speak about him to the crowds: 'What was the spectacle that drew you to the wilderness? A reed-bed swept by the
25 wind? No? Then what did you go out to see? A man dressed in silks and satins? Surely you must look in
26 palaces for grand clothes and luxury. But what did you go out to see? A prophet? Yes indeed, and far more than
27 a prophet. He is the man of whom Scripture says,

"Here is my herald, whom I send on ahead of you,
And he will prepare your way before you."

I tell you, there is not a mother's son greater than 28 John, and yet the least in the kingdom of God is greater than he.'

When they heard him, all the people, including the 29 tax-gatherers, praised God, for they had accepted John's baptism; but the Pharisees and lawyers, who refused his 30 baptism, had rejected God's purpose for themselves.

'How can I describe the people of this generation? 31 What are they like? They are like children sitting in the 32 market-place and shouting at each other,

"We piped for you and you would not dance."
"We wept and wailed, and you would not mourn."

For John the Baptist came neither eating bread nor 33 drinking wine, and you say, "He is possessed." The Son 34 of Man came eating and drinking, and you say, "Look at him! a glutton and a drinker, a friend of tax-gatherers and sinners!" And yet God's wisdom is proved right by 35 all who are her children.'

✶ The missions of John the Baptist and Jesus are very closely related in early Christian tradition. As this tradition developed one can see a tendency to present John as more and more conscious of his position as forerunner of the Messiah until, in John's Gospel, he explicitly points to Jesus as the 'Lamb of God' who takes away the sin of the world (John 1: 29, 36). This represents a tendency to dramatize and make plain the relationship which Jesus seems to have seen between John and himself. He let himself be baptized by John because he took the Baptist's summons to Israel to prepare for the messianic age as a 'sign' from the Father that this was the point at which he, Jesus, must begin his role in bringing in that age. Jesus himself saw this as a momentous decision; this is shown by the way he referred immediately to John the Baptist's mission when later on he was asked to identify himself. 'Tell us', said the priests, lawyers and elders, 'by what authority you are acting like this; who gave you this authority?' (Luke 20: 2). Jesus instantly put a counter-question, 'tell me, was the baptism of John from God or from men?' (Luke 20: 3–4). Jesus had had to come to the same sort of decision about taking John as a 'sign' from God as people have to make about Jesus. In Matthew and John, Jesus is recognized by the Baptist. In fact, as Mark and Luke suggest, when Jesus was baptized by John it is not likely that John knew who he was.

21–3. In Luke only is it mentioned that *there and then* Jesus performed some cures as a dramatic way of underlining the point of his answer to John. Luke also wishes to link this episode with the address of Jesus in the synagogue at Nazareth (4: 18). But it seems likely that the cures were taken as signs by Jesus himself. They were, so to speak, things he found happening to him as he set about to obey the Father's call rather than acts by which he deliberately decided to declare himself. Typically, in reply to a direct request to identify himself publicly, he returns an oblique but challenging answer. This seems to echo a number of passages in Isaiah concerning the messianic age: 'the eyes of the blind shall be opened' (35: 5); 'Then shall the lame man leap as an hart' (35: 6); 'the ears of the deaf shall be unstopped' (35: 5); 'the Lord hath anointed me to preach good tidings unto the meek' (61: 1). The healing of leprosy and the raising of the dead do not figure in the list of Old Testament signs of the messianic times, and Luke may have added them here because of the healing of the leper mentioned in 5: 12–16 and the raising of the widow's son at Nain just previously.

The 'signs', although real events, remained 'signs'. That is, how people responded to these events depended upon how far they were prepared to commit themselves in faith. They could equally well be 'signs' of the presence of a mere wonder-worker, or of demon-possession, or of the presence of Messiah. To take them as the latter might involve courage and repentance which a man was not willing to face; a real stumbling-block. But the Lord's blessing comes to those who have the courage and who do commit themselves in repentance.

24–35. The questions which Jesus here puts to the crowds were probably questions he had first put to himself. He does not ask them to make a choice that he has not faced himself. Neither he nor they had gone into the Judaean desert to look for things they were more likely to find somewhere else: the wind blowing through reeds at the waterside or a display of wealth. For Jesus, John was certainly a prophet, but a unique one, the last of the prophetic line, the one who ushers in the messianic age. Jesus once again obliquely implies that this age comes with himself.

27. Typically, Jesus presents himself indirectly as the Messiah. By identifying John as the herald mentioned in Mal. 3: 1 Jesus implies that the one who comes after this herald (Jesus himself) is none other than the Messiah.

28. The man who heralds the coming of the Messiah is unique, and unique for ever. John the Baptist is this person, Jesus implies. But there is a difference between a process which has reached its last stage but one and a process which has actually come to a head. A process which has come to a head is, just because it is a process, linked with what has gone before, but it is also a distinctive and new thing. Jesus implies (again notice his indirect manner) that this new and distinctive thing, the actual presence of the kingdom of God, is now there in himself and his disciples—for those with eyes willing to see such a thing.

29–30. These verses may not be the comment of the evangelist, as the text of the N.E.B. suggests, but part of the discourse of Jesus. If that is so Jesus is illustrating the point he has just been making. He is pointing to the ironical fact that ordinary people, even scoundrels such as the *tax-gatherers* were thought to be, had insight to see John as Jesus saw him, but religious leaders had not. Therefore, in the logic of Jesus, they denied that John was of any significance in the purpose of God.

31–4. The responses of his generation to John the Baptist and himself remind Jesus of children who in their games always want to win no matter what the rules may be. If the game goes against their particular wishes they will always find a reason to justify what they intend to do. So those who wish to come to no decision about John or Jesus, have easily found their reasons. John was an ascetic. They reject his asceticism as demon-possession, and so imply that they will accept someone who is not ascetic. But when Jesus shows that he is not, they reject him for that very reason.

34. It is not likely that Jesus spoke explicitly of himself as the Son of Man in this way. Originally he may have said 'I' here. In the handing down of the tradition the personal pronoun has become the explicit title.

35. There is another characteristic of children. Their unsophisticated insight enables them to perceive more quickly than others some things that are really important, just because they are less self-regarding. Examples of this now follow. ✳

FAITH AND FORGIVENESS

36 One of the Pharisees invited him to dinner; he went to the
37 Pharisee's house and took his place at table. A woman who was living an immoral life in the town had learned that Jesus was dining in the Pharisee's house and had
38 brought oil of myrrh in a small flask. She took her place behind him, by his feet, weeping. His feet were wetted with her tears and she wiped them with her hair, kissing
39 them and anointing them with the myrrh. When his host

the Pharisee saw this he said to himself, 'If this fellow were a real prophet, he would know who this woman is that touches him, and what sort of woman she is, a sinner.' Jesus took him up and said, 'Simon, I have 40 something to say to you.' 'Speak on, Master', said he. 'Two men were in debt to a money-lender: one owed 41 him five hundred silver pieces, the other fifty. As neither 42 had anything to pay with he let them both off. Now, which will love him most?' Simon replied, 'I should 43 think the one that was let off most.' 'You are right', said Jesus. Then turning to the woman, he said to Simon, 44 'You see this woman? I came to your house: you provided no water for my feet; but this woman has made my feet wet with her tears and wiped them with her hair. You gave me no kiss; but she has been kissing my 45 feet ever since I came in. You did not anoint my head 46 with oil; but she has anointed my feet with myrrh. And 47 so, I tell you, her great love proves that her many sins have been forgiven; where little has been forgiven, little love is shown.' Then he said to her, 'Your sins are for- 48 given.' The other guests began to ask themselves, 'Who 49 is this, that he can forgive sins?' But he said to the 50 woman, 'Your faith has saved you; go in peace.'

✶ Following on from the previous section the Pharisee in this story is presented as one who sees in Jesus, if not 'a glutton and a drinker', certainly a friend of sinners. The woman, on the other hand, immoral as her life may have been, had an openness and a capacity for self-giving which enabled her to see the way God's wisdom was working in Jesus.

37. In Christian tradition this woman has been identified with Mary of Magdala. This is because Mary of Magdala is

mentioned by Luke in the section immediately following this (8: 2) and is there described as one 'from whom seven devils had come out'. Further, in Mark 14: 3–9 and Matt. 26: 6–13 where there is a similar story about a woman anointing Jesus, the scene is, as here, the house of Simon. This traditional identification of the woman with Mary of Magdala is pure speculation.

38. It was usual for guests at a banquet like this to lie on a couch facing the table and leaning on one elbow. Jesus' feet would therefore be behind him, away from the table. The fact that the woman is said to have *wiped them with her hair* suggests that she had her hair let down and this was apparently a fashion amongst prostitutes at this time. To kiss someone's feet was a gesture expressing the most deeply felt gratitude.

39. In Luke's Gospel there is a use of irony very similar to the type which is used extensively in the Fourth Gospel. Christian readers of Luke's Gospel know that Jesus is not only 'a real prophet' but the 'Prophet-Messiah' who therefore, as John puts it, 'knew men so well, all of them, that he needed no evidence from others about a man, for he himself could tell what was in a man' (2: 24–5). This is another reminder to the reader that it is easy to miss the importance of Jesus, especially if one suffers from the kind of self-satisfaction and self-consciousness which Simon displays.

41–3. The point of this parable is that the generosity of love will be proportionate to the awareness of how much one has been forgiven. It is commonly suggested that there is a contradiction between the point of the parable and the actual case of the woman since her generosity of love precedes her forgiveness. This is not necessarily a difficulty. Professor Jeremias says: 'since it was a meritorious act to invite travelling teachers, especially if they had preached in the synagogue, to a Sabbath meal, we may at all events infer that before the episode which the story relates took place Jesus had preached a sermon which had impressed them all, the host, the guests, and an uninvited guest, the woman' (*The Parables of Jesus*,

p. 126). In that case Jesus might have shown in his sermon, as in the episode of the paralytic (5: 17–26), that forgiveness is not something he declares verbally by saying 'I forgive you', but something which comes in and through a person's response to him. Jesus therefore took the woman's uncalculating gratitude as a 'sign' that the Father had forgiven her. The use of the passive in *Your sins are forgiven* (verse 48) was a roundabout way (Jews regarding it as more reverent to avoid direct reference to God) of saying 'God has forgiven you'.

49. This question echoes the similar query on the occasion of the healing of the paralytic: 'Who but God alone can forgive sins?' (5: 21). *

PREACHING TOURS AND PARABLES

After this he went journeying from town to town and **8** village to village, proclaiming the good news of the kingdom of God. With him were the Twelve and a 2 number of women who had been set free from evil spirits and infirmities: Mary, known as Mary of Magdala, from whom seven devils had come out, Joanna, the wife 3 of Chuza a steward of Herod's, Susanna, and many others. These women provided for them out of their own resources.

People were now gathering in large numbers, and as 4 they made their way to him from one town after another, he said in a parable: 'A sower went out to sow his seed. 5 And as he sowed, some seed fell along the footpath, where it was trampled on, and the birds ate it up. Some 6 seed fell on rock and, after coming up, withered for lack of moisture. Some seed fell in among thistles, and the 7 thistles grew up with it and choked it. And some of 8 the seed fell into good soil, and grew, and yielded a hundredfold.' As he said this he called out, 'If you have ears to hear, then hear.'

9, 10   His disciples asked him what this parable meant, and he said, 'It has been granted to you to know the secrets of the kingdom of God; but the others have only parables, in order that they may look but see nothing, hear but understand nothing.

11   'This is what the parable means. The seed is the word of
12   God. Those along the footpath are the men who hear it, and then the devil comes and carries off the word from their hearts for fear they should believe and be saved.
13   The seed sown on rock stands for those who receive the word with joy when they hear it, but have no root; they are believers for a while, but in the time of testing they
14   desert. That which fell among thistles represents those who hear, but their further growth is choked by cares and wealth and the pleasures of life, and they bring
15   nothing to maturity. But the seed in good soil represents those who bring a good and honest heart to the hearing of the word, hold it fast, and by their perseverance yield a harvest.

16   'Nobody lights a lamp and then covers it with a basin or puts it under the bed. On the contrary, he puts it on a lamp-stand so that those who come in may see the light.
17   For there is nothing hidden that will not become public, nothing under cover that will not be made known and brought into the open.

18   'Take care, then, how you listen; for the man who has will be given more, and the man who has not will forfeit even what he thinks he has.'

19   His mother and his brothers arrived but could not get

to him for the crowd. He was told, 'Your mother and 20
brothers are standing outside, and they want to see you.'
He replied, 'My mother and my brothers—they are those 21
who hear the word of God and act upon it.'

✳ 1–3. This general comment is characteristic of Luke in its
particular mention of the fact that Jesus and the Twelve were
accompanied by *a number of women* who, now cured, provided
the money for the preaching tours.

2. To be possessed by *seven devils*, as Luke 11: 26 indicates
(the unclean spirit goes off and collects 'seven other spirits'),
means a case of extreme mental derangement.

3. *Joanna* (mentioned again in 24: 10) and *Susanna* are
names which occur only in Luke's Gospel. The fact that
Joanna's husband, *Chuza*, was *a steward of Herod's* is interesting
since it shows that Jesus had followers at the court of Herod
Antipas.

4–21. The parables of Jesus are often treated as if they were
all primarily illustrations of points in his teaching. It is
assumed that when he had illustrated his point in this striking
way everybody clearly understood. But the evidence shows
that the parables of Jesus, however vivid and arresting, were
not all illustrations; or if they were they clearly failed since
Jesus was asked, even by disciples, to give further explanations
of their meaning. The parables of Jesus may have had simplicity, but it was a simplicity which made more demands on
spiritual insight and readiness to repent than most people were
prepared to face.

The parables of Jesus were not always 'stories'; they could
be short sayings. The first parable in Luke to be named as
such, is the proverbial saying in 4: 23: 'Physician, heal yourself!' There is a variety of 'parables' in the Old Testament
and the use of parables is not unique to Jesus, although, as we
shall see, he did make use of them in a way which was
unique. In the Old Testament the word for 'parable'
(*māshāl*) is used to mean (1) a proverbial saying like 'Is Saul

also among the prophets?' (1 Sam. 10: 12; 19: 24); (2) an allegory, as in Ezekiel's parable of the two great eagles in 17: 2 ff.

For Jesus the 'parables' were 'signs' to be heard ('If you have ears to hear, then hear') just as the 'miracles' were 'signs' to be seen ('Happy are the eyes that see what you are seeing!'—Luke 10: 23). They were tokens, for those prepared to take them as such, that here in Jesus, in what he was saying and doing, God's messianic kingdom was being inaugurated. Many of the parables are therefore, as we shall see, allegorical presentations of the significance of Jesus, of his mission, and of his disciples.

4–8. In all three Synoptic Gospels the parable of the sower is addressed to crowds and has a certain prominence. This may be because it had come to be regarded as particularly characteristic of Jesus. It is a parable about the mission of Jesus in general, and therefore of key significance for understanding the meaning which he himself attached to his work. The secret coming of the kingdom of God in Jesus is like sowing seed. The sower knows that there will be waste, not everything he sows will grow to fruition. The extent of the harvest is not something he can settle; nevertheless he continues his work, confident that there will be a harvest. Listening to what Jesus has to say is more than a matter of physically hearing words, although of course it involves that. *Take care, then, how you listen* (8: 18).

8. Luke suggests that the seed which fell into good soil produced a perfect crop. Perhaps he disliked the suggestion in the Marcan tradition ('the yield was thirtyfold, sixtyfold, even a hundredfold', 4: 8) that even in favourable conditions the Lord's work might not come to full fruition.

9–10. This is a difficult saying because at first sight it looks as if Jesus is saying that the purpose of parables is the precise opposite of what most people suppose. They are not to make understanding easier by providing clear and arresting illustrations. They are to conceal and perplex.

The words of Jesus suggest that he has the call and commissioning of the prophet Isaiah in mind: 'Go, and tell this people, Hear ye indeed, but understand not; and see ye indeed, but perceive not' (6: 9).

The Greek word in verse 10 translated *in order that* is also frequently used in the New Testament to introduce quotations, and so the meaning is most probably to be taken as follows. In Luke's Gospel what Jesus says to crowds is frequently distinguished from what he said to disciples, and the evidence suggests that he made this distinction in actual fact. The disciples have inside knowledge about the kingdom of God; the very fact of their discipleship shows that they realize the kingdom is secretly present in what Jesus says and does. But this realization does not come superficially or automatically or by compulsion. The situation now, Jesus implies, is just as it was in Isaiah's time: what people hear and see, beyond the obvious and superficial, depends on what sort of persons they are. Have they the courage and discipline to act on certain things (words or actions) as signs from God with all that that involves in the way of faith, repentance, and surrender of self? This is one of many places which indicate that Jesus was greatly influenced, in determining the nature of his task, by the book of Isaiah.

11–15. Many scholars have felt that this interpretation of the parable of the sower cannot be the genuine words of Jesus. The reasons for this are as follows: (1) some think that allegory was only rarely a feature of the parabolic teaching of Jesus and a method of teaching more characteristic of the early Church, so much so that it is probable that an allegorical interpretation like this is the work of Christian teachers rather than of Jesus; (2) some of the words in this interpretation are thought to be more typical of the vocabulary of, say, Paul, than of Jesus; (3) to give 'explanations' after parables removes the purpose of parables as Jesus saw it, which is to summon to decision, a decision to which a man must come freely for himself and not after the kind of explanation which would leave him no option to dissent.

But against these three objections it can be argued: (1) That it is not at all apparent that allegory was a method of preaching which Jesus used only occasionally. If he saw his mission as a 'sign to be recognized', allegory is quite specially suited to the oblique and ironic manner which we have seen to be characteristic of Jesus' idea of the 'way of the Son of Man'. It allows the hearer freely to apply as much of it (or as little) to his own situation as he wishes (or dares). Allegory as a method is quite clearly used in such parables as the wicked vine-growers (Luke 20: 9-19), the two sons (15: 11-32) and the good Samaritan (10: 29-37). As we shall see when we come to these parables, Jesus used allegory to present the meaning both of his mission and of the discipleship which he saw resulting from it. This kind of allegorical parable we have already seen in Luke 5: 34-5: 'Can you make the bridegroom's friends fast while the bridegroom is with them? But a time will come: the bridegroom will be taken away from them, and that will be the time for them to fast.' (2) The words used in the 'explanation' are not so strikingly unusual as to make it impossible for Jesus to have used them. (3) This objection would be valid if it were an explanation to the crowds (who *have only parables*). But this explanation is given not to the crowds but to disciples, and it shows by what method Jesus believes he must give those outside the circle of disciples the means of making the free choice of faith.

The 'explanation' given by Jesus to the disciples suggests that the parable of the sower was the 'master' parable which gave the key to all the others. It is as near as Jesus *ever* comes to 'explaining' himself and his mission. The modifications which Luke makes reflect the evangelist's particular interpretation of the mission of Jesus. Jesus sees his mission as a way of speaking and acting which will give men the greatest opportunity to respond to the word of God. The devil will always be at hand to suggest plausible alternative explanations for genuine pointers to God; but keeping one's ears open to the word of God means to persist in loyalty and to be alert to the difficulties for faith which anxiety, affluence and pleasure bring.

14. In Luke *wealth and the pleasures of life* as such are presented as snares. In Mark (4: 19) and Matthew (13: 22) it is the 'false glamour of wealth' rather than wealth in itself which is warned against. Luke is more thoroughgoingly ascetic in his interpretation of the ministry and teaching of Jesus.

16–21. The parable of the sower suggests that Jesus believed that it was not likely that the Father would begin in his son's mission a process he did not mean to complete. The sower sows the seed given him, confident that there will be a harvest in spite of patches here and there where nothing happens. In further parabolic sayings Jesus makes the same point. If God has, in the mission of Jesus, lit a lamp, then one can rest assured that it will succeed in giving its light, even though there may be times during that mission when it looks as if its light has been completely covered over. The man with self-forgetfulness will find himself with the most insight into the meaning of Jesus, and to act on this insight brings the closest kinship to Jesus.

17. Jesus saw his mission as a 'sign'. It had a veiled incognito character. But disciples must have the same trust, to which he is committed, that in the end there will be an open revelation of what had previously only been alluded to.

19–21. This episode, which poses the questions 'Who is the mother of Jesus?' and 'Who are his brethren?' seems to have intrigued the author of John's Gospel, who takes up the theme and treats it with his own kind of irony. The closest kinship to Jesus is the result of obedient discipleship; Jesus and such true disciples are together intimately involved in obedience to the Father. The contrast between the absolute trust of Jesus and the lack of trust of the disciples is dramatically displayed in the following episode. *

THE STORM ON THE LAKE AND THE
GERGESENE PIGS

22 One day he got into a boat with his disciples and said to them, 'Let us cross over to the other side of the lake.'
23 So they put out; and as they sailed along he went to sleep. Then a heavy squall struck the lake; they began
24 to ship water and were in grave danger. They went to him, and roused him, crying, 'Master, Master, we are sinking!' He awoke, and rebuked the wind and the turbulent waters. The storm subsided and all was calm.
25 'Where is your faith?' he asked. In fear and astonishment they said to one another, 'Who can this be? He gives his orders to wind and waves, and they obey him.'

26 So they landed in the country of the Gergesenes,
27 which is opposite Galilee. As he stepped ashore he was met by a man from the town who was possessed by devils. For a long time he had neither worn clothes nor
28 lived in a house, but stayed among the tombs. When he saw Jesus he cried out, and fell at his feet shouting, 'What do you want with me, Jesus, son of the Most High God? I implore you, do not torment me.'

29 For Jesus was already ordering the unclean spirit to come out of the man. Many a time it had seized him, and then, for safety's sake, they would secure him with chains and fetters; but each time he broke loose, and with the devil in charge made off to the solitary places.
30 Jesus asked him, 'What is your name?' 'Legion', he replied. This was because so many devils had taken
31 possession of him. And they begged him not to banish them to the Abyss.

There happened to be a large herd of pigs nearby, 32
feeding on the hill; and the spirits begged him to let them
go into these pigs. He gave them leave; the devils came 33
out of the man and went into the pigs, and the herd
rushed over the edge into the lake and were drowned.

The men in charge of them saw what had happened, 34
and, taking to their heels, they carried the news to the
town and country-side; and the people came out to see 35
for themselves. When they came to Jesus, and found the
man from whom the devils had gone out sitting at his
feet clothed and in his right mind, they were afraid.
The spectators told them how the madman had been 36
cured. Then the whole population of the Gergesene 37
district asked him to go, for they were in the grip of a
great fear. So he got into the boat and returned. The 38
man from whom the devils had gone out begged leave
to go with him; but Jesus sent him away: 'Go back 39
home,' he said, 'and tell them everything that God has
done for you.' The man went all over the town spreading
the news of what Jesus had done for him.

* 22–5. According to this account Jesus seems to have
shared a common belief of the time that storms were the work
of demonic powers. He deals with the storm as he deals with
men possessed by demons. Some actual event in the ministry
lies behind this narrative. The point comes in the comment at
the end. Fear and lack of trust prevent men from recognizing
the lordship of Jesus. The next episode illustrates in a most
dramatic way the lordship of Jesus over the demonic forces
that plague human life.

26–39. This episode shows Jesus' mastery over the demons
that distress human beings. In spite of some features in this
narrative which seem to belong to the world of crude magic,

the fact that Jesus is asked to leave the area (all three synoptic evangelists agree that this was so) is a strong reason for believing that it is not all fiction. If a story of this kind had been entirely invented by early Christians, it would have ended with the crowd acclaiming Jesus. Luke, in fact, feels it necessary to explain why Jesus was asked to go: *for they were in the grip of a great fear* (8: 37). It is now impossible to discover exactly what happened. The many possibilities that have been suggested (that the pigs were frightened by the man's screams; that Jesus felt that in this case the man needed this proof that he was cured) only show that the actual facts are anybody's guess.

26. In Mark this district is called 'the country of the Gerasenes' (5: 1). In Matthew (8: 28) it is 'the country of the Gadarenes' in the best manuscripts, Gerasenes in others, and Gergesenes in yet others. In Luke the same three alternatives appear in the textual tradition, and on manuscript evidence the choice seems to be between Gergesenes and Gerasenes. The variant readings have grown out of attempts to get over the difficulty that the town of Gadara is not on the lakeside of the Sea of Galilee but six miles to the south-east. Gerasa was still farther to the south-east, some thirty miles, and so early readers must have felt that this was impossible as a locale for the incident. Gergesa seems to have been a suggestion of Origen who believed that such a place existed on the shore of the lake.

28. As in the case of the man possessed by a devil earlier (4: 34) this man is represented as having insight into the identity of Jesus. The fact that he shouts *son of the Most High God* may be meant to suggest that he is a Gentile because 'the Most High' was, according to the Jewish historian Josephus, a common title among Gentiles for the God of Israel.

30. Jesus seems to have shared the belief of the time that to defeat a demon it was essential to know his name. The 'name' of a person possessed a mysterious power in itself so that to get hold of it was half the battle.

31. Luke shows the demons of Legion making a desperate stand against being sent, defeated, into the 'Abyss' where the demons were kept. A description of this 'Abyss' is given in Rev. 9: 2 ff.

35. Luke pictures the healed man as sitting at the feet of Jesus. This is one of many places in this Gospel which suggest a tendency (more marked in John's Gospel) to present certain figures as illustrations of discipleship. Mary of Magdala (8: 2) 'from whom', says Luke, 'seven devils had gone out' is one such, and it looks as if this man is another.

39. It may be that Jesus saw this man as a sort of disciple and that whereas Mary of Magdala's role was to be one of those who travelled around with him, this man must go off to proclaim the 'Gospel to the Gentiles'. The content of his 'Gospel' is to be 'God's work in Jesus'. This is one more indication that Jesus took the healings which he found himself able to do as 'signs' from the Father that his mission was a disclosure of the kingdom of God. In this instance the kingdom involved the Gentiles. ✻

JAIRUS'S DAUGHTER AND THE WOMAN WITH HAEMORRHAGES

When Jesus returned, the people welcomed him, for they 40 were all expecting him. Then a man appeared—Jairus was 41 his name and he was president of the synagogue. Throwing himself down at Jesus's feet he begged him to come to his house, because he had an only daughter, about 42 twelve years old, who was dying. And while Jesus was on his way he could hardly breathe for the crowds.

Among them was a woman who had suffered from 43 haemorrhages for twelve years; and nobody had been able to cure her. She came up from behind and touched 44 the edge of his cloak, and at once her haemorrhage

45 stopped. Jesus said, 'Who was it that touched me?'
All disclaimed it, and Peter and his companions said,
'Master, the crowds are hemming you in and pressing
46 upon you!' But Jesus said, 'Someone did touch me, for
47 I felt that power had gone out from me.' Then the
woman, seeing that she was detected, came trembling
and fell at his feet. Before all the people she explained
why she had touched him and how she had been instantly
48 cured. He said to her, 'My daughter, your faith has cured
you. Go in peace.'

49   While he was still speaking, a man came from the
president's house with the message, 'Your daughter is
50 dead; trouble the Rabbi no further.' But Jesus heard,
and interposed. 'Do not be afraid,' he said; 'only show
51 faith and she will be well again.' On arrival at the house
he allowed no one to go in with him except Peter, John,
52 and James, and the child's father and mother. And all
were weeping and lamenting for her. He said, 'Weep no
53 more; she is not dead: she is asleep.' But they only
54 laughed at him, well knowing that she was dead. But
Jesus took hold of her hand and called her: 'Get up, my
55 child.' Her spirit returned, she stood up immediately,
56 and he told them to give her something to eat. Her
parents were astounded; but he forbade them to tell
anyone what had happened.

* The episode of the Gergesene pigs is followed by a closely
knit narrative about the raising of a *twelve*-year-old only
daughter and the healing of a woman with a *twelve*-year-old
haemorrhage. These uses of the number twelve are probably
deliberate, especially since the episodes which follow concern
the sending out of the twelve apostles, and the feeding of the

five thousand which resulted in the filling of *twelve great baskets* of scraps (Luke 9: 17). Number symbolism had an importance for Jesus and his contemporaries which it is difficult for us to appreciate. It is very probable that Luke (and indeed Jesus himself) may have taken the affair of the Gergesene pigs as a sign of the cleansing of the Gentiles from the Legion of devils whose home was now in the unclean pigs where they belonged (this is how a Jew would regard pigs). Now come signs that through Jesus 'the daughter of Zion' (as Israel was often called in the books of Isaiah and Jeremiah), typified by a twelve-year-old girl, will be restored, and another 'daughter' (8: 48), representing faithful Israel, will be healed.

41. The *president of the synagogue* was an official who was responsible for supervising the arrangements for worship.

44. Mark's description of the woman contains the statement (5: 26) that 'in spite of long treatment by doctors, on which she had spent all she had, there had been no improvement; on the contrary, she had grown worse'. The fact that Luke has omitted these details altogether supports the tradition that he was a doctor. As such he would find these details damaging to the medical profession. The insertion in some manuscripts of 'though she had spent all she had on doctors' before *nobody had been able to cure her* is most probably the result of some copyist wanting to bring Luke's account into line with Mark's Gospel.

The woman was obviously convinced, in a simple way, that it would be enough just to touch the clothes of Jesus.

46. This throws some light on the healing actions of Jesus. As the Gospel of John puts it, the works of Jesus are not entirely his own acts, although he is involved in them. They are the works of the Father. Jesus on this occasion shows he is aware of a power working through him. ✻

THE MISSION OF THE TWELVE

9 He now called the Twelve together and gave them power
and authority to overcome all the devils and to cure
2 diseases, and sent them to proclaim the kingdom of God
3 and to heal. 'Take nothing for the journey,' he told
them, 'neither stick nor pack, neither bread nor money;
4 nor are you each to have a second coat. When you are
admitted to a house, stay there, and go on from there.
5 As for those who will not receive you, when you leave
their town shake the dust off your feet as a warning to
6 them.' So they set out and travelled from village to
village, and everywhere they told the good news and
healed the sick.

* Jesus sent off the Twelve to speak and act in the same way
as himself: they are *to overcome all the devils and to cure diseases*,
as he has been doing, and, again like him, *to heal* and *proclaim
the kingdom of God*. Jesus seems to have regarded the setting up
of the kingdom of God as something which involved both
himself and the Twelve he had summoned to be associated
with him.

3. It is commonly assumed that Jesus' instructions about
what the Twelve are to take with them are concerned simply
with seeing that they travel with as little luggage as possible.
It is more probable, however, that Jesus saw their mission in
symbolic terms. A clue to what may have been in his mind is
given by Mark's account of what the Twelve must take on
their journey. This differs from Luke and Matthew in allowing
only two things for the journey, a stick and sandals. In Exod.
12: 11 the instructions for celebrating the Passover are: 'thus
shall ye eat it; with your loins girded, your *shoes* on your feet,
and your *staff* in your hand: and ye shall eat it in haste: it is the
Lord's passover.' Luke's Gospel suggests that Jesus saw his

whole mission as something of a pilgrimage journey up to
Jerusalem for Passover. Perhaps then he intended that his
Twelve should be seen as those who were tracing out a new
exodus similar to the journey commemorated in the Passover
celebration. And so those who *will not receive* them are to be
warned that they are rejecting more than mere casual passers-
by. In Luke, the disciples are not to take a stick and there is
no mention of shoes. Luke seems to have been less interested
at this point in the symbolism of the journey of the Twelve
and more interested in the ascetic poverty of the followers of
Jesus. *

MORE SPECULATION ABOUT JESUS, AND THE FEEDING OF THE FIVE THOUSAND

Now Prince Herod heard of all that was happening, and 7
did not know what to make of it; for some were saying
that John had been raised from the dead, others that 8
Elijah had appeared, others again that one of the old
prophets had come back to life. Herod said, 'As for 9
John, I beheaded him myself; but who is this I hear such
talk about?' And he was anxious to see him.

On their return the apostles told Jesus all they had done; 10
and he took them with him and withdrew privately to a
town called Bethsaida. But the crowds found out and 11
followed him. He welcomed them, and spoke to them
about the kingdom of God, and cured those who were in
need of healing. When evening was drawing on, the 12
Twelve approached him and said, 'Send these people
away; then they can go into the villages and farms round
about to find food and lodging; for we are in a lonely
place here.' 'Give them something to eat yourselves', 13
he replied. But they said, 'All we have is five loaves and

two fishes, nothing more—unless perhaps we ourselves are to go and buy provisions for all this company.'
14 (There were about five thousand men.) He said to his disciples, 'Make them sit down in groups of fifty or so.'
15, 16 They did so and got them all seated. Then, taking the five loaves and the two fishes, he looked up to heaven, said the blessing over them, broke them, and gave them
17 to the disciples to distribute to the people. They all ate to their hearts' content; and when the scraps they left were picked up, they filled twelve great baskets.

✻ 7–9. This passage makes clear the mysterious quality of the mission of Jesus; it could bear a wide variety of interpretation. For some he was John the Baptist risen, for others the coming Elijah and for others again a resurrected Old Testament prophet.

9. Luke simply mentions John the Baptist's death without going into the extensive detail which Mark and Matthew provide. This may be because he takes the view that Jesus was the Elijah. He is not therefore interested in the death of John the Baptist as a prefiguration of that of Jesus in the way that Mark seems to have been, judging from the way he has written a detailed account of the way the Baptist died.

10–17. The popular conception of this episode is a 'miraculous' multiplication of bread and fishes constituting an astonishing wonder story. Curiously enough there is no sign of bewilderment or astonishment on the part of those present. The remark of Jesus given, not in Luke but in Mark and Matthew (Mark 8: 19; Matt. 16: 9): 'When I broke the five loaves among five thousand, how many basketfuls of scraps did you pick up?' suggests that for Jesus this was not some obvious miracle, but a 'sign' that in Jesus and his followers sharing in this meal the messianic banquet is being held. Jesus frequently presents his mission as God's invitation to a banquet (Luke 15: 16–24). The *twelve great baskets* of scraps left over suggest that what this Messiah begins to give here he will continue to give to the new community, the new Israel, which he is creating.

16. This description of Jesus looking up to heaven (in prayer), *blessing* and breaking, and giving *to the disciples to distribute* probably influenced the way the early Church celebrated what was called 'breaking bread' (Acts 2: 46). ✻

PETER IDENTIFIES JESUS

One day when he was praying alone in the presence of his 18 disciples, he asked them, 'Who do the people say I am?' They answered, 'Some say John the Baptist, others 19 Elijah, others that one of the old prophets has come back to life.' 'And you,' he said, 'who do you say I am?' 20 Peter answered, 'God's Messiah.' Then he gave them 21 strict orders not to tell this to anyone. And he said, 'The 22 Son of Man has to undergo great sufferings, and to be rejected by the elders, chief priests, and doctors of the law, to be put to death and to be raised again on the third day.'

✻ Following the temptations, Jesus saw that his mission, in speech and action, had to be of such a kind that it challenged his contemporaries to a free decision without forcing the issue. Part of Jesus' obedience was to trust that as the Father would give him appropriate 'signs' from time to time, so too would he give to his hearers insight to recognize in his mission the coming of the kingdom of God. Peter is the first of the followers of Jesus to make the outright identification of Jesus as Messiah. Hitherto only the demons have done this. One might have expected the evangelist to add after Peter's reply something like 'You are right!' to underline for the reader the significance of this moment. But Luke is not that kind of propagandist. Instead he gives us a reply from Jesus which leaves us very uncertain whether 'Messiah' was a word Jesus would have used of himself, and introduces another cryptic theme: the necessary suffering of 'the Son of Man'.

18. As we should by now expect, Luke marks the special significance of this incident by a reference to the prayer of Jesus. Previous references of this kind are made at the baptism of Jesus (3: 21) and before the calling of the Twelve (6: 12).

19. The possible identities of Jesus suggested here are the same as those which Luke quotes as current rumours in 9: 7.

21–2. Instead of the usual Jewish pictures of the Messiah Jesus clearly preferred to set before his followers the mysterious figure of the 'Son of Man'. Jesus does not say that he is the 'Son of Man' in so many words, but he so uses the term in relation to his own mission as to suggest that he is the same person. The 'Son of Man' is one who *has to undergo great sufferings*. The phrase is strongly worded in the Greek. It means that the 'Son of Man' *must* suffer, not that he may perhaps, or even that he will be likely to suffer as political or other circumstances turn out. This is a 'must' for Jesus because he sees that his mission, designed by the Father, will be a living out of Israel's vocation to suffer. In the book of Daniel 'the son of man' (= the 'saints of the Most High' = Israel, 7: 13–14, 22, 27) has to suffer at the hands of others (7: 21). But in spite of humiliations and suffering Jesus trusts that the Father will as in the case of Daniel's 'son of man' bring the whole undertaking to a triumphant conclusion. There will be resurrection. Jesus believed that that was bound to come. There is no good reason to doubt that Jesus' trust in the Father was complete, and enabled him to see this coming. His recorded words about resurrection in the tradition are not necessarily inserted by others after the event.

on the third day means, as so often in the Old Testament, 'in a short time' (cf. Gen. 40: 13; Judg. 19: 4). *

THE SON OF MAN AND DISCIPLESHIP

And to all he said, 'If anyone wishes to be a follower of 23
mine, he must leave self behind; day after day he must
take up his cross, and come with me. Whoever cares for 24
his own safety is lost; but if a man will let himself be lost
for my sake, that man is safe. What will a man gain by 25
winning the whole world, at the cost of his true self?
For whoever is ashamed of me and mine, the Son of Man 26
will be ashamed of him, when he comes in his glory and
the glory of the Father and the holy angels. And I tell 27
you this: there are some of those standing here who
will not taste death before they have seen the kingdom
of God.'

✻ The pattern of the mission of Jesus, as 'Son of Man', is to
be the daily model for the disciple. It involves the same path
of self-conquest and participation in suffering.

23. In Mark's version of this saying the follower of Jesus
is summoned to 'take up his cross'; in Luke he is to do this
day after day. As originally spoken by Jesus the words may
have meant that discipleship is a most painful task because
it is self-giving and self-forgetting, like dragging a cross for
one's own execution. Mark may have taken the saying as a
summons to martyrdom. Luke believes that the Christian life
is a dying daily to self, much as Paul does in 1 Cor. 15: 31:
'Every day I die'. Later on Luke will picture Simon of Cyrene
literally fulfilling this summons of his Lord: 'they...put the
cross on his back, and made him walk behind Jesus carrying
it' (23: 26).

26. In a characteristically indirect way Jesus affirms that a
man's attitude to him and his disciples will determine the
reactions of the 'Son of Man' at the end of things. Instead of
me and mine some manuscripts have 'me and my words' but it

is nearer to the thought of Luke and Jesus himself to accept the text given here. As we have noticed, Jesus regarded himself and his disciples as together being used by the Father for the bringing in of his kingdom.

It looks as if, in this passage, Jesus was thinking of the Son of Man as some kind of advocate. He is to come in his own separate glory according to Luke, presumably to appear before the Father's glory and to plead on mankind's behalf.

27. Luke, of all the evangelists, comes nearest to making plain the idea that the coming of the kingdom of God is literally the coming of Jesus. He may therefore have taken this saying as an ironical suggestion by Jesus that the kingdom of God is really plain to see, to all those standing by, in Jesus himself, though only a few will have the faith to see it. The transfiguration which follows shows three of the disciples piercing in this way the 'incognito' of Jesus. ✳

THE TRANSFIGURATION

28 About eight days after this conversation he took Peter, John, and James with him and went up into the hills to
29 pray. And while he was praying the appearance of his face changed and his clothes became dazzling white.
30 Suddenly there were two men talking with him; these
31 were Moses and Elijah, who appeared in glory and spoke of his departure, the destiny he was to fulfil in Jerusalem.
32 Meanwhile Peter and his companions had been in a deep sleep; but when they awoke, they saw his glory and the
33 two men who stood beside him. And as these were moving away from Jesus, Peter said to him, 'Master, how good it is that we are here! Shall we make three shelters, one for you, one for Moses, and one for Elijah?'; but he spoke without knowing what he was saying.
34 The words were still on his lips, when there came a cloud

which cast a shadow over them; they were afraid as they
entered the cloud, and from it came a voice: 'This is my 35
Son, my Chosen; listen to him.' When the voice had 36
spoken, Jesus was seen to be alone. The disciples kept
silence and at that time told nobody anything of what
they had seen.

✻ Behind this episode there seems to lie an experience of three
prominent disciples which came to have the same kind of
significance for them as the experience following his baptism
had for Jesus. There is an obvious link between the two incidents in the words of the voice. 'Thou art my Son, my
Beloved' (3: 22) obviously pointed to an experience private to
Jesus. Here, *This is my Son, my Chosen; listen to him* equally
clearly points to an awareness of the meaning of Jesus which
came to Peter, John and James in a specially compelling way.

We have frequently noticed suggestions in the Gospel that
Jesus thought of his mission as something which the Father
was fashioning and moulding into a particular shape: an
embodiment of all that God had been saying, and of the way
he had been saying it, throughout the history of Israel. The
most likely explanation of this incident is that God, working
through the Spirit, as we should say now, enabled the three
disciples to see Jesus as the embodiment of all and more than
Moses and Elijah stood for, to see him in fact as the true Israel,
the chosen Son. To see Jesus in this way was to see him
transfigured.

This explanation is more probable than the notion that the
transfiguration story is based on an account of an appearance
of the risen Christ. Detailed examination shows that at point
after point this narrative differs strikingly from any of the
resurrection stories, so the suggestion raises more problems
than it solves.

28–9. This is the fourth major incident in the mission of
Jesus which Luke marks by a reference to Jesus praying. The

transfiguration in his Gospel actually takes place during prayer. The location is on the mountain.

30–1. There was a popular belief that Moses and Elijah had never died, and that both would reappear as forerunners of the messianic age. Jesus is seen to be a new and greater Moses and a new and greater Elijah, bringing to fruition Old Testament law and prophecy.

31. The Greek word translated *departure* and *destiny* is *exodos*. While it could mean 'death', more likely it indicates that the three became acutely aware that the whole direction of the mission of Jesus from Galilee up to Jerusalem was not a casual journey, but nothing less than a new exodus, with the consequence mentioned in the next verse.

32. Peter wants to mark the occasion by holding a feast of Tabernacles (in which the Jews lived in tent-like shelters for seven days as a way of re-enacting the exodus from Egypt and wanderings in the wilderness. See Lev. 23: 42–4). But it is wrong for Peter to want to keep Moses and Elijah in this way. He would be making Jesus just one more episode in the history of Israel; but Jesus *is* Israel personified, and it is time for Moses and Elijah to give way. What they had helped to create has appeared in the person of Jesus. ✳

AT THE FOOT OF THE MOUNT

37 Next day when they came down from the hills he was
38 met by a large crowd. All at once there was a shout from a man in the crowd: 'Master, look at my son, I implore
39 you, my only child. From time to time a spirit seizes him, gives a sudden scream, and throws him into convulsions with foaming at the mouth, and it keeps on
40 mauling him and will hardly let him go. I asked your
41 disciples to cast it out, but they could not.' Jesus answered, 'What an unbelieving and perverse generation! How

long shall I be with you and endure you all? Bring your
son here.' But before the boy could reach him the devil 42
dashed him to the ground and threw him into convulsions.
Jesus rebuked the unclean spirit, cured the boy, and gave
him back to his father. And they were all struck with 43
awe at the majesty of God.

Amid the general wonder and admiration at all he was
doing, Jesus said to his disciples, 'What I now say is for 44
you: ponder my words. The Son of Man is going to be
given up into the power of men.' But they did not 45
understand what he said; it had been hidden from them
so that they should not perceive its drift; and they were
afraid to ask him what it meant.

A dispute arose among them: which of them was the 46
greatest? Jesus knew what was passing in their minds, 47
so he took a child by the hand and stood him at his side,
and said, 'Whoever receives this child in my name receives 48
me; and whoever receives me receives the One who sent
me. For the least among you all—he is the greatest.'

'Master,' said John, 'we saw a man casting out devils 49
in your name, but as he is not one of us we tried to stop
him.' Jesus said to him, 'Do not stop him, for he who is 50
not against you is on your side.'

✻ After the transfiguration, Luke takes the reader back to the
situation where the significance of Jesus is once again a matter
of hints and guesses. The scene of distress and confusion at the
foot of the mountain of transfiguration may be intended to
recall the descent of Moses from the mount, where he had been
confronted with the glory of God, to the confusion of unbelief
below (see Exod. 32: 1–6 and 34: 29–35).

39. It is because of the symptoms mentioned here that the
boy in this incident is generally regarded as an epileptic.

41. The words of Jesus have an echo of well-known Old Testament passages which, because of their context, may have been in his mind on this occasion. In Num. 14: 11 God complains to Moses about the wilful refusal of the people to take on trust the 'signs' that he is doing for Israel: 'How long will this people despise me? and how long will they not believe in me, for all the signs which I have wrought among them?', and in Deut. 32: 5 Israel is described, for similar reasons, as 'a perverse and crooked generation'. This is one of many places where Jesus expresses his dismay that his contemporaries are taking the bodily cures as wonderful and welcome benefits and not as signs of the presence of something which demands repentance.

44. Jesus again (see 9: 22) refers to the destiny of *the Son of Man* but this time in less precise terms, and this may explain why the disciples found it so puzzling. This may well be the way Jesus originally referred to what lay ahead for *the Son of Man*.

45. Luke, writing some years later, no doubt found it difficult to understand why the disciples could not understand a saying that seemed clear enough to him, and here suggests that God had, for some reason, concealed the meaning from them. It is also possible to translate: 'But it was so obscure to them that they could not perceive its drift', in which case Luke is making no reference to God concealing the meaning.

46–8. Ironically, a dispute about greatness among the disciples breaks out immediately after the saying about the humiliating fate of the Son of Man! Where there is simplicity and humility there is Christ, and to act on this is an encounter with God.

49–50. The disciples of Jesus, as he had commanded, practised the casting out of devils, not always with success, as we have just seen in 9: 40. Casting out devils was not a preserve of the disciples or even of Jesus himself, as he points out: 'If it is by Beelzebub that I cast out devils, by whom do your own people drive them out?' (11: 19). The sort of possessiveness John displays is incompatible with discipleship. In the case of casting out devils disciples are to rejoice, not because *they* are responsible, but because 'your names are enrolled in heaven' (Luke 10: 20). In the long run it is not possible to misuse the name of Jesus for the driving out of demons. This is because to drive out demons, wherever it happens, is, for those with eyes to see, a sign of the conquest of the empire of evil, and so it belongs in fact to the work of Jesus' ministry. *

Journeys and Encounters

9: 51 — 18: 30

* So far, apart from chapters 2 and 3, Luke has, in the main, followed the general plan of Mark's Gospel, which he used as one of his sources. Now comes a long section, extending from 9: 51 to 18: 14, where Luke uses material not found in Mark. Clearly this is a deliberate piece of planning and it is worth spending some time trying to find out why Luke has in this section combined material from Q and his own sources in this particular way.

Luke, like other writers in the New Testament (John, and the authors of Hebrews and 1 Peter), has been powerfully influenced by the part played by the idea of journeying in Old Testament religion, and seems to have constructed his two books with this picture in mind. The mission of Jesus is in the form of a journey up to Jerusalem, but Luke (like John) seems to have taken this as a pointer to the journey of Jesus up to the Father in the ascension. That this is more than surmise is shown by the fact that the climax of Luke's Gospel is, deliberately, not the resurrection, but the ascension (24: 51). In his second volume, Acts, Christ journeys in a new way. By means of the Spirit he travels with his Christians from

Jerusalem to Rome. He even, as Spirit, directs the journey as at Acts 16: 6 f.

Comparison of this section with the structure of the book of Deuteronomy makes one think that Luke had at the back of his mind the journey of one of the 'old prophets', Moses, and the people of Israel to the borders of the promised land. As we have seen, in the temptation Jesus had a vision of himself brought to the top of Mount Pisgah to be shown the promised land (see note on 4: 2–13). And the question as he saw it then remains the same. Shall he go in and possess it by quick decisive means (e.g. by force), or leave it to the Father to bring him in as and when he will? The very first episode on this journey shows that, as with old Israel, there will be constant inducements to try to discover for certain 'whether the Lord is among us or not' (see Exod. 17: 7). Those nearest to Jesus, like James and John, will, with the best intentions, urge him to try to make things certain for himself. ✷

THE WANDERING SON OF MAN

51　AS THE TIME approached when he was to be taken up to heaven, he set his face resolutely towards
52　Jerusalem, and sent messengers ahead. They set out and went into a Samaritan village to make arrangements for
53　him; but the villagers would not have him because he
54　was making for Jerusalem. When the disciples James and John saw this they said, 'Lord, may we call down fire
55　from heaven to burn them up?' But he turned and
56　rebuked them, and they went on to another village.

57　As they were going along the road a man said to him,
58　'I will follow you wherever you go.' Jesus answered, 'Foxes have their holes, the birds their roosts; but the
59　Son of Man has nowhere to lay his head.' To another he said, 'Follow me', but the man replied, 'Let me go and

bury my father first.' Jesus said, 'Leave the dead to bury 60
their dead; you must go and announce the kingdom of
God.'

Yet another said, 'I will follow you, sir; but let me 61
first say goodbye to my people at home.' To him Jesus 62
said, 'No one who sets his hand to the plough and then
keeps looking back is fit for the kingdom of God.'

✻ These three incidents all give the impression that the
journey up to Jerusalem was of unique importance to Jesus.
Jerusalem, the Holy City, had a prominent place in the way the
men of the Old Testament pictured the future. Jerusalem was
the place where the Messiah would reign, the 'throne of
David'. It seems, then, that Jesus was now, as it were, acting
under special orders. The Father had indicated to him that the
move to kingship, whatever form that might take, must now
begin.

51. Luke deliberately puts, as a heading to this section, a
reminder that there is more to this journey of Jesus than going
to Jerusalem. It is already part of his ascension, *when he was
to be taken up to heaven*. According to Luke, Jesus showed
evidence of his conviction that it was an essential part of the
Father's 'must' for him that he should now begin his progress
to Jerusalem.

53. By the time of Jesus the long-standing tension between
Samaritans and Jews had become outright hostility and
separation. There were many reasons for this breach. After
the collapse of the northern kingdom in 722 B.C. the Assyrians
moved some of their own colonists into Samaria. Later on
the legend developed that all those who lived in Samaria were
of mixed blood (through inter-marriage) and therefore
racially inferior to the Jews. A similar legend developed
amongst the English in connexion with Australians. Because
it was the practice to deport prisoners to Australia the legend
grew that all Australians are descended from criminals. The

attitude of the Jews, following their return from the Babylonian exile, in excluding the Samaritans from Jerusalem was another reason for hostility. In the time of Jesus the Samaritans were a separate community (they still are) with their own temple and scriptures (the Pentateuch of the Old Testament only).

Jesus and his followers so obviously gave the impression of a pilgrimage to Jerusalem that the Samaritans were unwilling to co-operate.

54. As Jesus turned to make on behalf of Israel the return journey to Jerusalem he is faced with Israel's besetting sin, to demand assurances from God, having made up one's mind beforehand what sort of assurances will satisfy. Jesus was tempted, through his disciples, to act like Elijah and summon fire from heaven (2 Kings 1: 10f.) and thus provide such an assurance. Some manuscripts actually read here 'as Elijah did'. But as the transfiguration incident has shown Jesus is not one of the old prophets; he is the new Elijah and his mission is not to call for more signs, but to be the once-for-all sign himself. Jesus' explanation for this, given in some manuscripts, could well be a genuine saying of his: 'You do not know to what spirit you belong.' Jesus' own temptations have shown that it is the spirit of Satan which prompts the demand for self-satisfying certainty. The spirit of God involves turning to God and keeping alert for *his* signs.

57–8. To *follow* Jesus means very much more than simply to accompany him on a journey. This is a unique journey, nothing less than a special enactment of Israel's exodus, wanderings and entry into the promised land to which Jesus as the 'Son of Man', has set himself. 'Fox' seems to have been a word which Jews used to describe foreigners. Jesus calls Herod 'that fox' in Luke 13: 32. Again the Gentiles were frequently referred to as birds (based on passages like Ezek. 17: 23; 31: 6), and Jesus may have had this in mind in his reference to the birds of the air in the parable of the mustard-seed (Luke 13: 19).

The saying here may then mean: Israel's calling is to humiliation and service. Discipleship of the Son of Man, as Jesus embodies this calling in his own mission, involves always being on the move. Foreigners (foxes) and Gentiles (birds) can make their own kind of shelter, but Israel has no home of his own choosing.

60. It is very likely that there was an ironic ambiguity about Jesus' use of *dead* here; he uses 'dead' in two senses. The 'prodigal son' is described by Jesus as one who 'was dead' (15: 32). Just as Jesus has previously ironically asked, 'who are the virtuous people?' (5: 32) so now he ironically poses the questions: Who are the dead? Those who have died, or those who cannot recognize signs of life?

61–2. This saying of Jesus seems to have in mind Elijah's call of Elisha as recorded in 1 Kings 19: 19–20: 'Elisha the son of Shaphat...was ploughing....And he left the oxen, and ran after Elijah, and said, Let me, I pray thee, kiss my father and my mother, and then I will follow thee. And he said unto him, Go back again.' Discipleship is not something to be undertaken on impulse and without realizing what one is taking on. ✳

THE SIGN OF THE SEVENTY-TWO

After this the Lord appointed a further seventy-two and **10** sent them on ahead in pairs to every town and place he was going to visit himself. He said to them: 'The crop 2 is heavy, but labourers are scarce; you must therefore beg the owner to send labourers to harvest his crop. Be 3 on your way. And look, I am sending you like lambs among wolves. Carry no purse or pack, and travel 4 barefoot. Exchange no greetings on the road. When 5 you go into a house, let your first words be, "Peace to this house." If there is a man of peace there, your peace 6

will rest upon him; if not, it will return and rest upon
7 you. Stay in that one house, sharing their food and
drink; for the worker earns his pay. Do not move from
8 house to house. When you come into a town and they
9 make you welcome, eat the food provided for you; heal
the sick there, and say, "The kingdom of God has come
10 close to you." When you enter a town and they do not
11 make you welcome, go out into its streets and say, "The
very dust of your town that clings to our feet we wipe
off to your shame. Only take note of this: the kingdom
12 of God has come close." I tell you, it will be more
bearable for Sodom on the great Day than for that town.

13   'Alas for you, Chorazin! Alas for you, Bethsaida! If
the miracles that were performed in you had been
performed in Tyre and Sidon, they would have repented
14 long ago, sitting in sackcloth and ashes. But it will be
more bearable for Tyre and Sidon at the Judgement
15 than for you. And as for you, Capernaum, will you be
exalted to the skies? No, brought down to the depths!

16   'Whoever listens to you listens to me; whoever rejects
you rejects me. And whoever rejects me rejects the One
who sent me.'

17   The seventy-two came back jubilant. 'In your name,
18 Lord,' they said, 'even the devils submit to us.' He
replied, 'I watched how Satan fell, like lightning, out of
19 the sky. And now you see that I have given you the
power to tread underfoot snakes and scorpions and all the
forces of the enemy, and nothing will ever harm you.
20 Nevertheless, what you should rejoice over is not that
the spirits submit to you, but that your names are enrolled
in heaven.'

* It is often assumed that this second account of Jesus sending out disciples on a mission is simply Luke's adaptation of the sending out of the Twelve to symbolize the universal character of the work of Christ. If this is so we should have to say that Luke feels himself just as free to invent episodes to illustrate a point as some have thought John to be. That this incident is symbolic is certain, but it is the kind of symbolism which is so closely in keeping with the dramatic and symbolic character of so many of Jesus' actions at key points in his mission as to make it extremely probable that this was a deliberate gesture. What was for Jesus, in its inner meaning, a solemn procession of Israel up to Jerusalem for Passover began at Luke 9: 51. But, convinced now that the new Israel being formed through his movement included the Gentiles, he staged a symbolic demonstration that the gathering in of the Gentiles was now under way.

1. In some manuscripts the number given is 'seventy' and not *seventy-two*. Seventy, in the number symbolism of Judaism, was a conventional figure for all the nations of the world. Since Jesus was aware of himself as a kind of new Moses, he may also have had in mind Moses' appointment of seventy elders (Num. 11: 16). *Seventy-two* is the number given in the Greek translation of the Hebrew Old Testament, the Septuagint, for the nations of the world in Gen. 10, and Num. 11: 24, 26 seem to indicate seventy-two as the number of Moses' elders. Most probably this is the original reading, and 'seventy' crept in later because of its more common use as a symbol for something universal.

In this mission Luke sees a miniature representation of what is taking place in the mission of the Church as recorded in Acts. This may explain the fact that the seventy-two are sent out in pairs, but not the Twelve. The work of these pairs will be taken up later by Paul and Barnabas (Acts 13 ff.), Paul and Silas (Acts 15: 40) or Peter and John (Acts 8: 14).

2. Jesus very frequently thought of his mission as a harvesting. Interestingly, John's Gospel has a similar saying

('look, I tell you, look round on the fields; they are already white, ripe for harvest', John 4: 35) in connexion with the conversion of Samaritans.

3. Israel, and especially Israel among the Gentiles, was frequently compared to a lamb (for example, Isa. 53: 7) and one of the marks of the 'age to come' was that 'the wolf shall dwell with the lamb' (Isa. 11: 6).

4. Their journey was a symbol of what was happening in the coming of Jesus rather than a properly prepared mission in its own right. It was a gesture which Jesus wanted given quickly. There was no time to stop and pass the time of day!

5–6. There will be those who are morally alert enough to recognize what is going on and they will receive the good things the Gospel brings. Others will miss it, but nevertheless the Gospel is something that comes not only with Jesus but also with those whom he has sent.

8–9. Two things are to be done as 'signs': one in action and one in word. The first is to heal the sick, as Jesus had done, and the second to proclaim that *the kingdom of God has come close to you*, as Jesus also had done. This suggests that Jesus saw the mission of the seventy-two as an extension of his own.

10–11. The mission of the seventy-two was of such a kind that people ought to recognize its meaning. Not to accept it was a case of grave error in judgement. Jesus saw it as a rejection of the Father's friendly gesture in bringing the kingdom to them.

12. The reference is to the story in Genesis 19. Sodom became in Jewish tradition a by-word for ingrained evil. Jesus thought of his generation as being in worse case than Sodom. Sodom did not have the opportunities for repentance that are being given to the contemporaries of Jesus.

13–15. Jesus thinks of the reaction to his own mission as similar to the consequences of rejecting those whom he sends. He refers to a phase of his ministry which he obviously regarded as important though no details of it have come down in the tradition. From what Jesus says here it seems that he did not regard the *miracles* as extraordinary happenings to astonish people, but summonses to repentance. *Tyre* and *Sidon*, again by-words for heathenism and wickedness, had not had the privileges of this generation, and *Capernaum* seemed irredeemably self-satisfied!

16. This was the important principle underlying Jesus' attitude to the Twelve and the seventy-two. He and they were so intimately linked with the one coming of the kingdom of God that to receive an apostle was tantamount to receiving Jesus himself.

17–20. Again an important passage for understanding the imagination of Jesus and his attitude to 'miracles'. The report that the demons were submitting to those whom he had sent out was a dramatic sign that his mission was being used for the conquest of evil. We may rightly infer that this was also how he took the healings in his own ministry of those possessed by demons. They were tokens that the Father was at work in his mission. If his followers were to rejoice it must be not because the casting out of devils showed their own power, but because it showed that their Father, and his, was with them.

This further example of Jesus' poetic imagination and use of imagery makes it unlikely that he meant the reference to the power *to tread underfoot snakes and scorpions* to be taken literally. It was soon taken literally, as one of the secondary endings of Mark's Gospel (16: 18) or the episode of Paul and the viper (Acts 28: 3–6) shows. It is still taken literally by some American snake-handling sects. In fact Jesus most probably had in mind Ps. 91: 13:

Thou shalt tread upon the lion and adder:
The young lion and the serpent shalt thou trample under
feet

and used this image to suggest the coming in his mission of the victory over all the powers of evil. ✳

JESUS AND THE FATHER

21 At that moment Jesus exulted in the Holy Spirit and said, 'I thank thee, Father, Lord of heaven and earth, for hiding these things from the learned and wise, and revealing them to the simple. Yes, Father, such was thy choice.'

22 Then turning to his disciples he said, 'Everything is entrusted to me by my Father; and no one knows who the Son is but the Father, or who the Father is but the Son, and those to whom the Son may choose to reveal him.'

23 Turning to his disciples in private he said, 'Happy the
24 eyes that see what you are seeing! I tell you, many prophets and kings wished to see what you now see, yet never saw it; to hear what you hear, yet never heard it.'

✻ Luke again points to the special significance of this episode by putting it explicitly in the context of the action of the Spirit. Certainly it was one of those points in the ministry where Jesus revealed something of his self-awareness, and it ought to be studied alongside the accounts of his baptism and the confession of Peter at Caesarea Philippi. He hints at being in a uniquely intimate relation to God as Father, and yet does not identify himself explicitly.

The words of Jesus in this passage are thought by some to be so like the kind of language ascribed to him in John's Gospel and so unlike his manner of speech in the Synoptic Gospels that the whole episode has been described as 'a Johannine thunderbolt in the synoptic sky'. This is not self-evident. Jesus elsewhere in the synoptic tradition, as for example at the baptism, showed that he felt his relation with God as Father in a specially intimate and unique way, a relationship which, in Semitic fashion, he here expresses in terms of knowledge. Hebrew uses the verb 'to know' of sexual intercourse, and 'knowledge' of God in Hebrew continued to have this association of intimate personal reciprocal relationship. This use of 'know' has come into English through the Bible. Further, the sense that upon him rested a special commission from the Father was a feature of the mission of Jesus as a whole.

21. Jesus gives thanks to the Father that his way of revealing himself is through 'signs', which the unsophisticated can seize hold of, and not through puzzles which only the clever can solve. Jesus rejoices that understanding God's love does not demand mental qualities which not all may possess.

22. *Everything is entrusted to me* would suggest, in the idiom of the Jews of Jesus' day, a teacher entrusting knowledge to a pupil. It looks as if Jesus, conscious of being uniquely Son, is aware that this involves learning from the Father like a pupil. Perhaps Jesus saw in his instruction of the disciples a representation of the Father's instruction of him.

The tense of the Greek verb translated *is entrusted* makes it likely that some specific event is being referred to when the Father's particular 'tuition' of the Son began. This may well be the baptism of Jesus; if so, we have here further light on how Jesus himself saw this event. After the baptism the Father handed over to Jesus, the Son, the commission to introduce the kingdom of God in a visible way in himself, his acts, his words, his disciples.

no one knows who the Son is. Jesus, as an embodiment of Israel, is God's Son and what this means in the purpose of God is something only the Father fully knows.

23–4. The mission of Jesus as a whole had a pattern. Those whose consciences were alert would be able to recognize it. This pattern contained all the features of the messianic age indicated in the Old Testament. ✻

THE PARABLE OF THE GOOD SAMARITAN

25 On one occasion a lawyer came forward to put this test question to him: 'Master, what must I do to inherit
26 eternal life?' Jesus said, 'What is written in the Law?
27 What is your reading of it?' He replied, 'Love the Lord your God with all your heart, with all your soul, with all your strength, and with all your mind; and your neigh-
28 bour as yourself.' 'That is the right answer,' said Jesus; 'do that and you will live.'

29 But he wanted to vindicate himself, so he said to Jesus,
30 'And who is my neighbour?' Jesus replied, 'A man was on his way from Jerusalem down to Jericho when he fell in with robbers, who stripped him, beat him, and went
31 off leaving him half dead. It so happened that a priest was going down by the same road; but when he saw
32 him, he went past on the other side. So too a Levite came to the place, and when he saw him went past on the
33 other side. But a Samaritan who was making the journey came upon him, and when he saw him was moved to
34 pity. He went up and bandaged his wounds, bathing them with oil and wine. Then he lifted him on to his own beast, brought him to an inn, and looked after him there.
35 Next day he produced two silver pieces and gave them to the innkeeper, and said, "Look after him; and if you spend any more, I will repay you on my way back."
36 Which of these three do you think was neighbour to the
37 man who fell into the hands of the robbers?' He answered, 'The one who showed him kindness.' Jesus said, 'Go and do as he did.'

✻ The theme of discipleship, which has been the particular subject of the evangelist since he turned to narrate the journey to Jerusalem, lies behind this passage containing the parable of the good Samaritan. The question put to Jesus asks, in fact, 'What is a disciple?' and the answer is 'One who obeys the Law'. Of course to ask a question about discipleship is to ask who Jesus is. This kind of *test question* always faced Jesus with the temptation to make an outright reply as if he, rather than the questioner, were the right person to identify his mission. Characteristically the reply of Jesus, both directly to the lawyer and in the parable, is ambiguous and leaves the questioner to come to his own decision. The lawyer is shown that he already has the key to the right answer. He must now see what obedience to the Law has to do with following Jesus. In the allegorical way which best suited the indirect reply he had to give, Jesus asks the man 'Who is in fact doing the Law? Those who are concerned with the ritual details of the Law, like priests and Levites, or an outsider like the Samaritan who had a clear eye for a neighbour's need?' This necessarily poses the question 'Is Jesus the Samaritan who really obeys the Law, though unconventionally, and is discipleship of him an imitation of his manner?' That is left to the questioner.

25. A lawyer was a person educated in the Jewish Law and its interpretation. The nearest equivalent in modern Judaism would be a rabbi. Apart from the interpretation of the Law, the lawyers acted as judges in the courts and, specially interesting for this passage, trained young men in discipleship.

27. This reply is a combination of Deut. 6: 5: 'thou shalt love the Lord thy God with all thine heart, and with all thy soul, and with all thy might' and Lev. 19: 18: 'thou shalt love thy neighbour as thyself'. It is a combination which Jesus himself uses in Mark 12: 29–31, and it may well be that it had been made before the time of Jesus. In the 'Testament of Issachar', for example (one of the *Testaments of the Twelve Patriarchs* which some scholars have dated around 100 B.C., although it should be remembered that other scholars think

this work is of Christian origin), we find 'Love the Lord and your neighbour'. What is distinctive about the teaching of Jesus is not that its details are all new. Rather it points to his person, work and words as a unique fulfilment, in human life, of the task of Israel to obey the Law and walk in 'the way of the Lord'.

30. Contact with blood or corpses made one 'unclean' according to the Jewish Law. Hence touching this man would involve a technical breach of ritual regulations.

31–2. Jewish priests performed the traditional religious ceremonies of Judaism. The Levites held various administrative positions in the temple and also assisted in giving instruction in the Law and tradition.

33. The Samaritan had become a symbol of everything that was foreign to Judaism for the reasons given in the note on 9: 53. Moreover, the Samaritan, because completely unclean in the eyes of Jews, was the only one who could without breaking the Law, that is, without defilement, help a man whose wounds (or corpse) would give a priest, Levite, or any strict Jew a lot of trouble ceremonially. Thus he is like Jesus who, having courageously associated with the 'unclean' prostitute or leper had rendered himself 'unclean' but had helped them by doing so.

34. The use of wine for cleaning wounds and oil for soothing them seems to have been quite common in ancient medical practice. Alcohol is antiseptic.

36–7. As so often with his parables Jesus leaves his listeners to apply the situation of the story to themselves. The 'neighbour' could be the Jew who is helped by the *Samaritan* (an unwelcome thought for Jews!), or he could be the Samaritan who is quicker to see human need than the morally correct *priest* or *Levite*. Either way it seems to involve Jews behaving like Samaritans! ✳

TYPES OF DISCIPLE

While they were on their way Jesus came to a village 38
where a woman named Martha made him welcome in
her home. She had a sister, Mary, who seated herself at 39
the Lord's feet and stayed there listening to his words.
Now Martha was distracted by her many tasks, so she 40
came to him and said, 'Lord, do you not care that my
sister has left me to get on with the work by myself?
Tell her to come and lend a hand.' But the Lord answered, 41
'Martha, Martha, you are fretting and fussing about so
many things; but one thing is necessary. The part that 42
Mary has chosen is best; and it shall not be taken away
from her.'

* Jesus sees in the different reactions of the two women a
parable of discipleship. Mary is the example of those who can
see that Jesus is himself the Law and are ready to be instructed
by him. Martha lacks the kind of attention which brings
insight. Mary is praised by Jesus, perhaps in accordance with
the principle which he had expressed in Luke 8: 18: 'the man
who has [attention] will be given more [insight]'.

38–9. Only Luke provides this information about two
sisters named Martha and Mary. This is another of his links
with the material used in John's Gospel where the two sisters
reappear, with their brother Lazarus.

41–2. Mary seems a model of the ideal disciple who can
perceive in the words of Jesus something of overriding significance, what John in his Gospel would have thought of
as discerning the 'Word' of God in the 'words' of Jesus. *

PRAYER TO THE FATHER

11 Once, in a certain place, Jesus was at prayer. When he
ceased, one of his disciples said, 'Lord, teach us to pray,
2 as John taught his disciples.' He answered, 'When you
pray, say,

> "Father, thy name be hallowed;
>   Thy kingdom come.
3   Give us each day our daily bread.
4   And forgive us our sins,
>   For we too forgive all who have done us wrong.
>   And do not bring us to the test."'

5   He added, 'Suppose one of you has a friend who comes
to him in the middle of the night and says, "My friend,
6 lend me three loaves, for a friend of mine on a journey
has turned up at my house, and I have nothing to offer
7 him"; and he replies from inside, "Do not bother me.
The door is shut for the night; my children and I have
gone to bed; and I cannot get up and give you what you
8 want." I tell you that even if he will not provide for
him out of friendship, the very shamelessness of the
request will make him get up and give him all he needs.
9 And so I say to you, ask, and you will receive; seek, and
10 you will find; knock, and the door will be opened. For
everyone who asks receives, he who seeks finds, and to
him who knocks, the door will be opened.
11   'Is there a father among you who will offer his son a
12 snake when he asks for fish, or a scorpion when he asks
13 for an egg? If you, then, bad as you are, know how to
give your children what is good for them, how much

more will the heavenly Father give the Holy Spirit to those who ask him!'

✻ Two versions of the Lord's Prayer have come down to us in the New Testament; the one here and another in the Sermon on the Mount in Matthew (6: 9–13). In Matthew it is in a context dealing with prayer in general. Here in Luke, characteristically, it comes after one of Jesus' periods of prayer and in a context concerned with discipleship. In Luke, Jesus is presented more explicitly as the model of the Christian disciple's prayer, and, as we shall note in the comments, there is evidence for thinking that the shape of the Lord's Prayer reflects the pattern of Jesus' own life of prayer. There are signs that very soon this prayer came to occupy an important place in Christian worship. The prayer of praise (doxology) to be found at the end of the prayer in some manuscripts of Matthew, 'For thine is the Kingdom and the power and the glory, for ever. Amen' suggests that by the time Matthew was written the Lord's Prayer was being used in worship. Again the structure of the prayer of Jesus in John, chapter 17, seems to have been influenced by the framework of the Lord's Prayer. At the same time we need to remember that Mark obviously thought it possible to give the bare essentials of what Jesus did and said without including the Lord's Prayer.

2. Originally it seems that Jesus began the prayer with simply *Father* rather than 'Our Father in heaven' as Matthew has it. Some manuscripts of Luke, clearly influenced by Matthew, give the longer form. There are two reasons for thinking that the original prayer began simply *Father*. One is that Matthew has a general tendency in his Gospel to use the longer phrase (common in contemporary Jewish prayers) 'Your father in heaven', etc. The other and more important reason is that there is evidence that God as Father was such a unique and intimate reality to Jesus that there was, so to speak, a characteristic tone of voice in his references to the Father. This would explain why the actual Aramaic word which he

used ('Abba') has been retained in the Gospel tradition. In Gethsemane he prayed 'Abba' (Father) (Mark 14: 36), and when Paul talks about Christians, because of their relationship with Christ, being able to address God as Father with a new realization of what it is to be sons, he says that they are enabled, through the Spirit, to cry 'Abba! Father!' (Rom. 8: 15). Palestinian Jewish practice then, as now, is to use 'father', by itself, of one's parent. For God a possessive pronoun and a more roundabout phrase is used (like 'our Father in heaven'). Jesus was therefore saying 'father' to God in an unusual and startlingly intimate way. For the early Christians, saying 'Father' in prayer was more than simply repeating the word after Jesus. It took them to the very heart of their religion and, indeed, to the centre of Jesus' own awareness of God. It was only through their relationship with Christ that they could share in his intimate address to God, his Father (through his unique sonship) and theirs (as a result of their discipleship). For Jesus the Fatherhood of God was not something to be taught in words, but a reality to be detected through his mission of obedient sonship.

thy name be hallowed is a phrase very frequently found in Jewish prayers, but there can be no doubt that giving glory to God has a special meaning for Jesus. It was the task of his mission to do just this. John's Gospel in fact presents the mission of Jesus as a 'glorifying' of the Father. The *name* of God in Jewish tradition meant very much more than the actual word God. The name of a person in the Old Testament is not only his means of identification but includes his character, his family background and ancestry, nationality, race, and social status. The *name* of God means then both the mystery of the being of God and all that he has shown himself to be in history and experience. For Jesus hallowing this name was the duty of every man, a duty which affected his day-to-day living. Some indication of his profound reverence for the *name* of God can be seen in his remarks to the rich man (Luke 18: 19) or his reaction to swearing (Matt. 5: 33–7).

The rich man is told not to use 'good' in a glib thoughtless manner, because goodness is part of the nature of God and no one, not even Jesus, is good by accident. Therefore one cannot properly talk about goodness without having God in mind. In the same way Matthew's record of Jesus' comments on swearing suggests that Jesus saw a man's use of words as a sign of the range of his reverence: 'You are not to swear at all—not by heaven, for it is God's throne, nor by earth, for it is his footstool, nor by Jerusalem, for it is the city of the great King, nor by your own head, because you cannot turn one hair of it white or black.'

The disciple will pray that he may follow Jesus in this profound reverence for the Father.

Jesus himself was aware that the coming of the kingdom of God in a unique way was taking place during his mission, and also that this process would have its finale in the future when the whole mysterious working of God's kingship was disclosed. The disciples are to pray likewise that the kingdom which has come in Jesus will be brought to fruition.

Some manuscripts have instead of *Thy kingdom come* 'Thy Holy Spirit come upon us and cleanse us'. This may well be what Luke wrote and what Jesus actually said. This Gospel brings out the significance of Jesus and his mission as a work of the Spirit. There is evidence that Jesus was himself aware of this endowment by the Spirit although he did not speak about it directly because this would have been the kind of self-advertisement which he avoided. Perhaps because this alternative reading was associated with a notorious early Christian heretic, Marcion, the more conventional and acceptable version *Thy kingdom come* gained ground. Some manuscripts insert from Matthew 'Thy will be done, On earth as in heaven', while one has a version which contains elements of both traditions: 'thy kingdom come upon us'.

If the petition for the Spirit is genuine it indicates that the disciple must pray for the Spirit, here again following the pattern of his Lord.

3. *Give us each day our daily bread* is the most difficult clause in the Lord's Prayer because of the uncertainty about the meaning of the Greek word translated *daily*. There are two main suggestions. The first is that the word was originally used for the daily rations handed out to soldiers, slaves and workmen. In this case the petition is in line with Jesus' teaching about anxiety in Matt. 6: 34, 'do not be anxious about tomorrow; tomorrow will look after itself'.

The other suggestion is that Jesus is still thinking of the future and the prayer is for the bread of the future, 'our bread for the morrow', and is another way of saying *Thy kingdom come*. There is evidence that it was understood in this way in the early Church.

It is significant that the imagery of bread and loaves chiefly occurs in situations of temptation. There is Jesus' own temptation to 'tell this stone to become bread' (Luke 4: 3), and his reaction to the declaration of the disciples 'We have no bread' following the Pharisees' seeking a 'sign from heaven' (Mark 8: 11). In John's Gospel the parallel to this petition in the Lord's Prayer ('Sir, give us this bread now and always', 6: 34) again occurs in a context about signs: 'What sign can you give us to see, so that we may believe you?' (6: 30). The people ask for a sign to give them their own kind of certainty at the very moment that a sign is being given to them—Jesus himself, the bread of life.

Once again the prayer of the disciple is to be like that of the Master. As Jesus lived in the confidence that the Father would bring in the kingdom so must they. In Luke the daily drill of the Christian includes taking up the cross ('day after day', Luke 9: 23) and, as here, reaffirming one's entire dependence upon God.

4. In the sermon on the 'level ground' Jesus had said to his disciples: 'you must love your enemies and do good...and... you will be sons of the Most High, because he himself is kind to the ungrateful and wicked' (6: 35). The same truth is now expressed in a different way in the Lord's Prayer. To forgive

those who have wronged us is unquestionably an imitation, in human terms, of how God deals with us. Once again, in the perspective of the Gospel as a whole, Luke presents Jesus as the model for Christians, this time of the forgiveness of those who do one an injury. For those who crucify him Jesus prays, in Luke's gospel, 'Father, forgive them; they do not know what they are doing' (23: 34).

Faith involves courage, insight and obedience. From one angle the life of faith is bound to appear a series of tests which may produce a spirit of 'Oh, what's the use?' and 'I shan't bother if it's going to be hard'. Indeed Jesus himself saw his mission as a sequence of tests ('You are the men who have stood firmly by me in my times of trial', 22: 28). But, as is made plain at Gethsemane, God enables one to face such times of trial. He enables victory over Satanic temptations. This appears in Matthew's version of the Lord's Prayer (Matt. 6: 13) which has influenced the texts of some manuscripts of Luke which add here 'But save us from the evil one'.

5–8. Jesus' aim in his parables is to enable the listener freely to find his own way to faith from reflection on observation or experience. If, he argues, we in our self-regard can be brought to help our fellow-men at the cost of great inconvenience, how much more likely it is that God, who is self-giving not self-regarding love, will meet our needs. Prayer must consistently and insistently be made with this truth in mind.

9–10. This passage (9–13) is in verse form. The incantatory effect of the language indicates that the nearness of the Father and his utter readiness to forgive were such unquestionable realities to Jesus that endless persistence in prayer is a natural rhythm of life.

11–13. Another good example of Jesus' use of the argument from analogy. Some genuine features of fatherhood constantly appear in human life in spite of sin and selfishness. Although we cannot know what God's 'fatherhood' is like, we can safely assume that it is not less generous than the love

that a human father can display. It includes the gift of the
Holy Spirit which enables one to see, among other things,
Jesus as the sign of the kingdom come. This is the subject of
the next section of the Gospel. *

THE SIGN OF THE CROSS

14 He was driving out a devil which was dumb; and when
the devil had come out, the dumb man began to speak.
15 The people were astonished, but some of them said,
'It is by Beelzebub prince of devils that he drives the
16 devils out.' Others, by way of a test, demanded of him a
17 sign from heaven. But he knew what was in their
minds, and said, 'Every kingdom divided against itself
18 goes to ruin, and a divided household falls. Equally if
Satan is divided against himself, how can his kingdom
stand?—since, as you would have it, I drive out the devils
19 by Beelzebub. If it is by Beelzebub that I cast out devils,
by whom do your own people drive them out? If this
20 is your argument, they themselves will refute you. But
if it is by the finger of God that I drive out the devils,
then be sure the kingdom of God has already come upon
you.
21   'When a strong man fully armed is on guard over his
22 castle his possessions are safe. But when someone
stronger comes upon him and overpowers him, he carries
off the arms and armour on which the man had relied
and divides the plunder.
23   'He who is not with me is against me, and he who does
not gather with me scatters.
24   'When an unclean spirit comes out of a man it wanders
over the deserts seeking a resting-place; and finding none,

it says, "I will go back to the home I left." So it returns 25
and finds the house swept clean, and tidy. Off it goes and 26
collects seven other spirits more wicked than itself, and
they all come in and settle down; and in the end the man's
plight is worse than before.'

While he was speaking thus, a woman in the crowd 27
called out, 'Happy the womb that carried you and the
breasts that suckled you!' He rejoined, 'No, happy are 28
those who hear the word of God and keep it.'

With the crowds swarming round him he went on to 29
say: 'This is a wicked generation. It demands a sign,
and the only sign that will be given to it is the sign of
Jonah. For just as Jonah was a sign to the Ninevites, so 30
will the Son of Man be to this generation. At the Judge- 31
ment, when the men of this generation are on trial, the
Queen of the South will appear against them and ensure
their condemnation, for she came from the ends of the
earth to hear the wisdom of Solomon; and what is here is
greater than Solomon. The men of Nineveh will appear 32
at the Judgement when the men of this generation are on
trial, and ensure their condemnation, for they repented at
the preaching of Jonah; and what is here is greater than
Jonah.

'No one lights a lamp and puts it in a cellar, but rather 33
on the lamp-stand so that those who enter may see the
light. The lamp of your body is the eye. When your eyes 34
are sound, you have light for your whole body; but when
the eyes are bad, you are in darkness. See to it then that the 35
light you have is not darkness. If you have light for your 36
whole body with no trace of darkness, it will all be as
bright as when a lamp flashes its rays upon you.'

✶ Jesus believed that his speech and actions had to be of such a kind that they would enable the Father to use them as tokens of his setting up the kingdom of God. To demand *a sign from heaven* showed that those who asked for such a clear demonstration were incapable of seeing the true tokens which God was actually giving. In fact by taking the actions of Jesus as signs not *from heaven* but from below ('*It is by Beelzebub prince of devils that he drives the devils out*') they were making it quite clear that the only signs which they would regard as *from heaven* would be those which made no moral or spiritual demands, and confirmed their own view of themselves.

15. The derivation and meaning of *Beelzebub* are uncertain. It might mean 'Lord of flies' or 'Lord of dung'. Clearly it was a name of abuse attached to the chief of the demons and in verse 18 Jesus seems to identify him with Satan.

17–20. Who Jesus is and by what authority he acts is not for him to say. '*Every kingdom divided against itself goes to ruin, and a divided household falls*' is an enigmatic parable, according to Mark (3: 23), which those who hear it must solve. It is for his contemporaries to decide one way or the other. The driving out of devils is not indisputable evidence of the presence of the kingdom of God. As far as appearances go it could equally well be evidence of the presence of the kingdom of Satan. It depends on whether one is prepared to see here *the finger of God*. The latter phrase seems an echo of Exod. 8: 17–19 where the Egyptian magicians recognize in the action of Moses 'the finger of God' but Pharaoh, whose heart remained 'hardened', did not. Jesus asks his hearers to consider whether history is repeating itself. Once again, the signs of the God of Israel are missed by those to whom they are principally addressed.

19. 'Driving out devils' was such a frequent, even ordinary, happening that there is nothing indisputably divine or messianic about Jesus' actions, taken in isolation. The question is: Is there something special about *his* doing them?

21–2. This parable requires its hearers to decide whether in

Jesus they can see the *someone stronger* whose work involves the mastery of evil. It is a typically indirect messianic announcement.

23. This saying is again a challenge to see in Jesus the gatherer-together of scattered Israel. One of the marks of the messianic age, according to the Old Testament, is the unifying of the people of God.

24–6. Jesus suggests that there is very much more to the fact that he drives out demons than just another astonishing cure of the kind which was a commonplace of the day (see verse 19). The cure only enables the man to make a rational free decision. One way or other he must decide, otherwise the will and the capacity to decide will go. Then the last state will be worse than the first, because the man will have brought this paralysis of the will on himself.

27–8. There are times in the Gospel of John when it looks as if the evangelist thinks of the mother of Jesus as being in one way Mary but in another way faithful and humble Israel. Here in Luke, and also in Mark (3: 32–5), there is some evidence that Jesus himself used 'mother' in this twofold way. In Mark, when told that his mother is outside asking for him, his reply is 'Who is my mother?' and he then identifies her as those who do the will of God. Similarly, here he implies that his mother can be represented by *those who hear the word of God and keep it.* Later on Christians were to make great use of the idea that Christ is born again in the lives of those who are loyal to his Gospel.

29–32. In speaking of this generation as *wicked* in demanding a sign Jesus has in mind faithless Israelites who kept on prescribing to God the only kind of signs they would regard as satisfactory. This, as Jesus saw in the temptation, is a blasphemous attempt to tell God what to do. God does give signs, but they are real signs, like that of Jonah, and allow genuine freedom to respond (or not to respond). The preaching of Jonah was a sign, for those morally ready to take it, of the need for moral renewal. The Ninevites did see it like that, and repented, just as the Queen of Sheba took Solomon as a sign of the presence of God's wisdom for her time and generation. Jesus' generation is confronted with something greater than this. What that is he characteristically does not say, but the response to his actions which he looks for is not superficial astonishment but repentance, and the latter is appropriate only in the presence of God. Jesus implies therefore that to be faced with him is to be in the presence of God.

33–6. Again, as in the Gospel of John, perception of the meaning of Jesus is indicated by the imagery of light and seeing, and rejection of Jesus by their opposites. Courage to act and spiritual alertness alone give the insight which is required for perceiving in what Jesus does and says 'signs' of God. *

ON PHARISEES AND LAWYERS

37 When he had finished speaking, a Pharisee invited him to
38 dinner. He came in and sat down. The Pharisee noticed with surprise that he had not begun by washing before
39 the meal. But the Lord said to him, 'You Pharisees! You clean the outside of cup and plate; but inside you
40 there is nothing but greed and wickedness. You fools! Did not he who made the outside make the inside too?
41 But let what is in the cup be given in charity, and all is clean.

42 'Alas for you Pharisees! You pay tithes of mint and rue and every garden-herb, but have no care for justice and the love of God. It is these you should have practised, without neglecting the others.

43 'Alas for you Pharisees! You love the seats of honour in synagogues, and salutations in the market-places.

44 'Alas, alas, you are like unmarked graves over which men may walk without knowing it.'

In reply to this one of the lawyers said, 'Master, when 45 you say things like this you are insulting us too.' Jesus 46 rejoined: 'Yes, you lawyers, it is no better with you! For you load men with intolerable burdens, and will not put a single finger to the load.

'Alas, you build the tombs of the prophets whom your 47 fathers murdered, and so testify that you approve of the 48 deeds your fathers did; they committed the murders and you provide the tombs.

'This is why the Wisdom of God said, "I will send 49 them prophets and messengers; and some of these they will persecute and kill"; so that this generation will have 50 to answer for the blood of all the prophets shed since the foundation of the world; from the blood of Abel to the 51 blood of Zechariah who perished between the altar and the sanctuary. I tell you, this generation will have to answer for it all.

'Alas for you lawyers! You have taken away the key 52 of knowledge. You did not go in yourselves, and those who were on their way in, you stopped.'

After he had left the house, the lawyers and Pharisees 53 began to assail him fiercely and to ply him with a host of questions, laying snares to catch him with his own words. 54

⋆ The Pharisees were a group within Judaism who first came into prominence during the second century B.C. They were laymen anxious to spread the Jewish way of life as a definite and strict discipline covering the whole of human activity. In some ways they were a 'puritan' party within Judaism and one suggested meaning for 'Pharisee' is 'separated'. Others have thought that the name has something to do with 'Persian' because many of the ideas of the

Pharisees, as for instance some of their beliefs in the after-life, may have been of Persian origin. Believing that religion is related to the whole of life they attempted to interpret the Law so as to cover the entire range of human affairs. In doing so they ran the risk of becoming harsh and insensitive. It was this element in Pharisaism that Jesus criticized.

42. The nature of Jesus' criticism of the Pharisees must obviously have turned on the tone of voice used in these sayings. But even as to words it is worth remarking that Jesus actually said, as the N.E.B. translation makes clear, *Alas for you Pharisees*, and not, as is sometimes assumed, 'A curse on you Pharisees!' There is a satirical note in many of his pictures of the Pharisees, as here, but it is not negative or destructive satire. There is a remedial note in it, which suggests that if the Pharisees would get their finicky obsession with tiny details into perspective, they would be able to distinguish the important from the trivial.

The saying *It is these you should have practised, without neglecting the others* is not in some manuscripts. It may have crept into the others because it occurs in a similar passage in Matthew (23: 23).

44. Graves were thought to have a defiling influence on anyone who touched them (see Num. 19: 16: 'whosoever... toucheth...a grave, shall be unclean seven days'). To help people not to walk on them without meaning to, graves were often whitened. This is the practice referred to in Matthew's version of the saying: 'You are like tombs covered with whitewash' (23: 27).

45. The *lawyers* were professional students or teachers of the Law (also called 'scribes' in the New Testament). Not all of them were Pharisees, but as theorists about the Law which the Pharisees aimed to obey rigorously, criticism aimed at the Pharisees naturally involved them.

46. The lawyers' interpretation of the Law did not simplify it, and learned jargon was allowed to overshadow the needs of the ordinary person.

47–51. Jesus thought of the prophets as a line of martyrs
and no doubt felt that as one who belonged to this tradition
his mission was likely to end in a martyr-like death. One of
the marks of the Old Testament prophet was his belief that
he had been caught up by God, however momentarily or
spasmodically, into a real glimpse of the purpose or 'counsel'
of God. Behind this passage there seems to be Jesus' awareness
that he has been granted a uniquely intimate vision of the
purpose of God in sending his spokesmen to Israel. This
purpose has, Jesus now implies, come to a head in his own
time, and he thinks it likely that the Old Testament history
of prophecy from the murder of Abel (Gen. 4) to the killing
of Zechariah (2 Chron. 24—2 Chronicles is the last book of
the Hebrew Bible) will be repeated in a way that will place
his own generation under special judgement.

52. Throughout his ministry Jesus showed himself specially
sensitive to unnecessary handicaps placed on simple folk who
had not the education to fend for themselves. The lawyers
had been producing the kind of theology which gets in the
way of ordinary religion. ✶

MORE ON DISCIPLESHIP

Meanwhile, when a crowd of many thousands had **12**
gathered, packed so close that they were treading on one
another, he began to speak first to his disciples: 'Beware
of the leaven of the Pharisees; I mean their hypocrisy.
There is nothing covered up that will not be uncovered, 2
nothing hidden that will not be made known. You may 3
take it, then, that everything you have said in the dark
will be heard in broad daylight, and what you have
whispered behind closed doors will be shouted from the
house-tops.

'To you who are my friends I say: Do not fear those 4

who kill the body and after that have nothing more they
5 can do. I will warn you whom to fear: fear him who,
after he has killed, has authority to cast into hell. Believe
me, he is the one to fear.

6 'Are not sparrows five for twopence? And yet not one
7 of them is overlooked by God. More than that, even the
hairs of your head have all been counted. Have no fear;
you are worth more than any number of sparrows.

8 'I tell you this: everyone who acknowledges me before
men, the Son of Man will acknowledge before the angels
9 of God; but he who disowns me before men will be
disowned before the angels of God.

10 'Anyone who speaks a word against the Son of Man will
receive forgiveness; but for him who slanders the Holy
Spirit there will be no forgiveness.

11 'When you are brought before synagogues and state
authorities, do not begin worrying about how you will
12 conduct your defence or what you will say. For when the
time comes the Holy Spirit will instruct you what to say.'

✳ 2–3. The saying of Jesus: *There is nothing covered up that
will not be uncovered, nothing hidden that will not be made known*
occurs in a number of different contexts which vary the
meaning. In Mark (4: 22) it relates to the secret and open
coming of the kingdom; in Matthew it becomes an exhorta-
tion to disciples to utter publicly what Jesus has said privately;
here in Luke the reference is to the coming of judgement
when the defects of Pharisaism will be disclosed.

4. Disciples, those initiated into the secrets of Jesus, are his
friends. This is another link between a theme in Luke and
what we find in John: 'I have called you friends, because I
have disclosed to you everything that I heard from my Father'
(John 15: 15).

5. Jesus speaks of the *fear* of God as well as of the love of God. There is the fear that fetters a man (usually, at bottom, springing from some kind of self-concern) and the fear that liberates him (the fear of hurting or hindering love). Jesus sees life as a matter of serious moral decisions which have eternal consequences. We need not be too serious about our own judgements; we cannot take God's judgement too seriously.

This saying throws some light on what the Incarnation involved. Jesus does not impose on his disciples orders or burdens which he has not faced himself. The author of the Letter to Hebrews sees one of the significant features of Jesus to be his consistent 'godly fear'.

6–7. Again an indication of the depth of Jesus' own trust. The man who has little trust is usually cautious about saying that God cares in detail for the whole of life. The trust which Jesus has is such that he does not shrink from saying that God cares for the smallest detail.

8–9. A typical example of the oblique way in which Jesus indicates his relation to the *Son of Man*. The *Son of Man* is present in Jesus in a mysterious way, so that reactions to Jesus will count as reactions to the *Son of Man* when the latter figure is fully disclosed.

10. The original context of this saying is most likely to have been that in which it recurs in Mark, namely the Beelzebub controversy (Mark 3: 28–9). Mistaken abusive language about the *Son of Man* is forgivable (it may spring from honest and genuine conviction) but not slandering the Holy Spirit by ascribing (as in the charge 'It is by Beelzebub prince of devils that he drives the devils out', Luke 11: 15) the works of Jesus to the devil. This kind of argument could only come from a person who had so perverted normal insight and commonsense as to make forgiveness impossible. Forgiveness is not magic but has to be rationally understood and willingly received.

11–12. Jesus will be the perfect model of this teaching in his bearing during the trial. In Acts Luke gives many examples of the Spirit being given in just the circumstances Jesus here alludes to. See the account of Stephen's behaviour before the Jews in Acts 6: 8 — 8: 1. *

THE HAZARDS OF WEALTH

13 A man in the crowd said to him, 'Master, tell my brother
14 to divide the family property with me.' He replied, 'My good man, who set me over you to judge or
15 arbitrate?' Then he said to the people, 'Beware! Be on your guard against greed of every kind, for even when a man has more than enough, his wealth does not give him
16 life.' And he told them this parable: 'There was a rich
17 man whose land yielded heavy crops. He debated with himself: "What am I to do? I have not the space to store
18 my produce. This is what I will do," said he: "I will pull down my storehouses and build them bigger. I will
19 collect in them all my corn and other goods, and then say to myself, 'Man, you have plenty of good things laid by, enough for many years: take life easy, eat, drink, and
20 enjoy yourself.'" But God said to him, "You fool, this very night you must surrender your life; you have made
21 your money—who will get it now?" That is how it is with the man who amasses wealth for himself and remains a pauper in the sight of God.

* 13-14. Jesus was obviously taken by this man to be a rabbi, and, as was customary, he was asked to give a legal decision on a dispute with his brother. But the mission of Jesus is not to give legal judgements, to judge in that sense, but to be the means whereby God shows how he judges. Verses 8-9 have just made it clear that judgement is contained in the coming of Jesus and men's reactions to it. This theme

is taken up in John: 'It was not to judge the world that God
sent his Son into the world, but that through him the world
might be saved' (3: 17).

15. Envy and greed are self-regarding attempts to render
oneself immune from the kind of judgement that comes with
Jesus. This is a judgement that concerns more than the distri-
bution of property—it is the serious judgement of a man's
life, as in the parable which follows in verses 16–21. ✳

FREEDOM FROM ANXIETY

'Therefore', he said to his disciples, 'I bid you put away 22
anxious thoughts about food to keep you alive and clothes
to cover your body. Life is more than food, the body 23
more than clothes. Think of the ravens: they neither sow 24
nor reap; they have no storehouse or barn; yet God feeds
them. You are worth far more than the birds! Is there a 25
man among you who by anxious thought can add a foot
to his height? If, then, you cannot do even a very little 26
thing, why are you anxious about the rest?

'Think of the lilies: they neither spin nor weave; yet 27
I tell you, even Solomon in all his splendour was not
attired like one of these. But if that is how God clothes 28
the grass, which is growing in the field today, and tomorrow is thrown on the stove, how much more will
he clothe you! How little faith you have! And so you 29
are not to set your mind on food and drink; you are not
to worry. For all these are things for the heathen to run 30
after; but you have a Father who knows that you need
them. No, set your mind upon his kingdom, and all the 31
rest will come to you as well.

'Have no fear, little flock; for your Father has chosen 32

33 to give you the Kingdom. Sell your possessions and give
in charity. Provide for yourselves purses that do not wear
out, and never-failing wealth in heaven, where no thief
34 can get near it, no moth destroy it. For where your
wealth is, there will your heart be also.

✻ 22–3. The saying assumes that basic food and clothing are
available, and that it is getting things disastrously out of
proportion to be too worried about them.

24–8. These verses are in poetic form. Jesus takes the two
images of birds and flowers as examples of a natural dependence upon God which men ought to imitate. In detail,
the image of the ravens is less successful in making the point
since ravens *do* work in collecting food and building shelter,
and many of them die of hunger. But the image has its own
truth, as a picture of carefree dependence, even if it is not to be
applied in every detail.

27. The words 'they grow, they do not toil or spin' have
crept into some manuscripts, perhaps influenced by the
corresponding version in Matthew (6: 28).

28. A repetition of Jesus' belief that men are right to argue
from the fact that God is lavish in the way he works in
nature to the probability that he will be still more generous
to human beings.

29–31. Jesus warns against the sort of worry which is
caused by concern with ourselves and which causes us to be
imprisoned in a world of our own narrow interests. This
false outlook must go before we can see that God and his
purpose are the only things that ultimately matter.

32. The fact that Jesus so frequently uses the imagery of
shepherd and sheep when speaking either of God's purpose,
or of the disciples, shows that he regards his followers as a
messianic community in the making. To them is given the
kingdom (Jesus himself?).

33. Luke alone records Jesus giving this order to his

followers to sell their possessions and he sees this carried out in the early Church (Acts 2: 44–5; 4: 32–5). Other evidence in Luke suggests that while in one particular case Jesus required this action (the ruler in Luke 18: 18–23), in another case he allowed a man to continue with his wealth (Zacchaeus, Luke 19: 1–10)—or at least half of it! (see 19: 8). In view of the passage which follows, the warning about wealth may have sprung from Jesus' belief not only that it is dangerous because it easily becomes an obsession, but also that it is an encumbrance in view of the nearness of the appearance of the 'Son of Man'. ✳

DISCIPLES IN THE INTERVAL

'Be ready for action, with belts fastened and lamps alight. 35 Be like men who wait for their master's return from a 36 wedding-party, ready to let him in the moment he arrives and knocks. Happy are those servants whom the 37 master finds on the alert when he comes. I tell you this: he will buckle his belt, seat them at table, and come and wait on them. Even if it is the middle of the night or 38 before dawn when he comes, happy they if he finds them alert. And remember, if the householder had known 39 what time the burglar was coming he would not have let his house be broken into. Hold yourselves ready, 40 then, because the Son of Man is coming at the time you least expect him.'

Peter said, 'Lord, do you intend this parable specially 41 for us or is it for everyone?' The Lord said, 'Well, who 42 is the trusty and sensible man whom his master will appoint as his steward, to manage his servants and issue their rations at the proper time? Happy that servant who 43 is found at his task when his master comes! I tell you 44 this: he will be put in charge of all his master's property.

45 But if that servant says to himself, "The master is a long time coming", and begins to bully the menservants and
46 maids, and eat and drink and get drunk; then the master will arrive on a day that servant does not expect, at a time he does not know, and will cut him in pieces. Thus he will find his place among the faithless.

47 'The servant who knew his master's wishes, yet made no attempt to carry them out, will be flogged severely.
48 But one who did not know them and earned a beating will be flogged less severely. Where a man has been given much, much will be expected of him; and the more a man has had entrusted to him the more he will be required to repay.

* For Luke, as we shall see, the first signs of the *parousia* (the coming of the 'Son of Man') have come with the resurrection. For Jesus himself signs of the final stages of God's bringing in the kingdom were evident during the mission. His disciples, commissioned to do what he did, live in the interval before the whole process is finished, and they must be ready for this at any moment.

37. This parable of the master's return from a wedding-party and the giving of another feast is an allegorical presentation of the Son of Man's return (verse 40), as the bridegroom (verse 36) or the servant (verse 37) for the messianic banquet with the Twelve.

39–40. Another parable suggesting the surprise character of the coming of the *Son of Man*. Compare 1 Thess. 5: 2, 'the Day of the Lord comes like a thief in the night'.

41. Peter asks whether the banquet is literally only for the Twelve, or for everybody. This is one of a number of places where members of the Twelve think of the coming of the kingdom in terms of privilege for themselves, as, for example, the favour asked by James and John in Mark 10: 35–40. Jesus

replies by suggesting that this is a wrong question. What
matters is loyalty, and readiness, and if the Twelve are
privileged recipients of the kingdom that only means that a
deeper faithfulness will be required of them. They must
follow the way of Jesus who is himself the faithful servant. *

DECIDING ON THE SIGNS OF THE TIMES

'I have come to set fire to the earth, and how I wish it 49
were already kindled! I have a baptism to undergo, and 50
how hampered I am until the ordeal is over! Do you 51
suppose I came to establish peace on earth? No indeed,
I have come to bring division. For from now on, five 52
members of a family will be divided, three against two
and two against three; father against son and son against 53
father, mother against daughter and daughter against
mother, mother against son's wife and son's wife against
her mother-in-law.'

He also said to the people, 'When you see cloud bank- 54
ing up in the west, you say at once, "It is going to rain",
and rain it does. And when the wind is from the south, 55
you say, "There will be a heat-wave", and there is.
What hypocrites you are! You know how to interpret the 56
appearance of earth and sky; how is it you cannot
interpret this fateful hour?

'And why can you not judge for yourselves what is the 57
right course? While you are going with your opponent 58
to court, make an effort to settle with him while you are
still on the way; otherwise he may drag you before the
judge, and the judge hand you over to the constable, and
the constable put you in jail. I tell you, you will not come 59
out till you have paid the last farthing.'

* Verses 49–53 are in poetic form and give further insight into the creative imagination of Jesus.

49. Jesus, like John the Baptist, uses the Old Testament image of fire as a metaphor of judgement (see note on 3: 16–17). But while he is certain that his mission means the bringing in of the kingdom, and therefore of judgement, his role is like that which he has just outlined for his disciples: loyalty and obedience when there is every temptation to force the issue by taking everything into one's own hands. The fire is not his to kindle personally (compare his rebuke to James and John who wanted to call down fire from heaven to burn up the Samaritan villagers, 9: 54), but nevertheless it comes with him. The Father will kindle the fire. The nature of the judgement that has been going on in Jesus will, Jesus is convinced, be unveiled in Jerusalem. In the Gospel of John the crucifixion is such a revelation.

50. Jesus speaks of his task as *a baptism*. This is not baptism in the Christian sense but is rooted in the Old Testament picture of suffering and calamity as a being plunged under the waves:

> Then the waters had overwhelmed us,
> The stream had gone over our soul:
> Then the proud waters had gone over our soul.
>
> (Ps. 124: 4–5)

Jesus longs for the end but it is not for him to fix the time. His mission involves a tragic necessity which he accepts, a facing of death as a forbidding ordeal.

51–5. An ironical utterance of Jesus because in the perspective of this Gospel he certainly comes to bring peace (cf. 2: 14, 'on earth his peace for men on whom his favour rests' and 19: 42, 'If only you [Jerusalem] had known, on this great day, the way that leads to peace!'). The peace which Jesus brings is not the quiet of apathy but the serenity of devoted discipleship.

54–6. The 'signs' of the times are not trick puzzles which only a few can solve. They are of a kind that men ought to recognize, as they do indications of the coming weather. What is required is not a special sort of cleverness, but the insight which self-disregard brings into being, as the following parabolic sayings show.

57-9. Normal ability to see what is right should lead men to see the urgent necessity of coming to a decision about Jesus. His mission is like serving a bankruptcy charge on his contemporaries. If men who are in debt know how to act before the situation becomes unmanageable, we should be able to see how much wiser it would be for us (who are debtors to God) to get the debt settled in the way God himself indicates. Matthew (5: 25-6) uses these sayings to illustrate the general need for reconciliation. ✶

SUFFERING, SIN AND A LAST CHANCE
FOR ISRAEL

At that very time there were some people present who **13** told him about the Galileans whose blood Pilate had mixed with their sacrifices. He answered them: 'Do 2 you imagine that, because these Galileans suffered this fate, they must have been greater sinners than anyone else in Galilee? I tell you they were not; but unless you 3 repent, you will all of you come to the same end. Or the 4 eighteen people who were killed when the tower fell on them at Siloam—do you imagine they were more guilty than all the other people living in Jerusalem? I tell you 5 they were not; but unless you repent, you will all of you come to the same end.'

He told them this parable: 'A man had a fig-tree 6 growing in his vineyard; and he came looking for fruit on it, but found none. So he said to the vine-dresser, "Look 7 here! For the last three years I have come looking for

fruit on this fig-tree without finding any. Cut it down.
8 Why should it go on using up the soil?" But he replied,
"Leave it, sir, this one year while I dig round it and
9 manure it. And if it bears next season, well and good; if
not, you shall have it down."'

* 1–3. This is the only reference in the Gospels to this
incident and from what we know of Pilate's dislike of Jews
from writers like Josephus and Philo, some massacre of
Galilean Jews at the temple in Jerusalem may well have been
ordered by Pilate. Jesus rejects the idea, common in the Old
Testament, that such a happening must be a judgement on the
sin of those who were killed; this is no solution of the problem
of suffering. He takes up the subject of judgement. We
should be less willing to believe that the misfortunes of others
are a judgement on their sin, and more ready to believe that it
might be true of ourselves. In making these remarks Jesus
may have had in his mind the fall of Jerusalem and the horrors
of the Jewish war of A.D. 66–70, which he saw as a coming
judgement.

6. The fig-tree is a common symbol of Israel in the Old
Testament: 'I saw your fathers as the firstripe in the fig tree
at her first season' (Hos. 9: 10).

7–9. This may be an allegorical parable indirectly pointing
to the nature of the mission of Jesus. This way of referring to
the meaning of what he was doing was a method which
Jesus believed to be in keeping with the Father's will. He
speaks of his mission in the same allegorical way in the parable
of the vineyard tenants in Luke 20: 9–16. Jesus thinks of
God looking for fruit (a response to Jesus) on the fig-tree
(Israel) just as Isaiah had pictured God looking for grapes in his
vineyard (Israel) (Isa. 5: 1–7). Jesus was reluctant to believe
that Israel's final answer would be no, as his lament in verses
34–5 shows. Perhaps he saw this journey to Jerusalem as one
last attempt to win Israel, but the next episode does not augur
well. *

A DAUGHTER OF ABRAHAM

One Sabbath he was teaching in a synagogue, and there 10, 11
was a woman there possessed by a spirit that had crippled
her for eighteen years. She was bent double and quite
unable to stand up straight. When Jesus saw her he called 12
her and said, 'You are rid of your trouble.' Then he laid 13
his hands on her, and at once she straightened up and
began to praise God. But the president of the synagogue, 14
indignant with Jesus for healing on the Sabbath, inter-
vened and said to the congregation, 'There are six work-
ing-days: come and be cured on one of them, and not on
the Sabbath.' The Lord gave him his answer: 'What 15
hypocrites you are!' he said. 'Is there a single one of you
who does not loose his ox or his donkey from the manger
and take it out to water on the Sabbath? And here is this 16
woman, a daughter of Abraham, who has been kept
prisoner by Satan for eighteen long years: was it wrong
for her to be freed from her bonds on the Sabbath?'
At these words all his opponents were covered with 17
confusion, while the mass of the people were delighted
at all the wonderful things he was doing.

* Jesus' action in restoring one of their own people should
have indicated to the Jews that here was one who was lord
of the Sabbath and who had the mastery over Satan—but
they can see nothing more than one who breaks the Sabbath,
though in a way which they themselves were ready to
countenance! If they had had eyes to see they would have
recognized in this incident a sign that, in Jesus, God is de-
feating evil. Furthermore, God's victorious campaign never
stops, not even on the Sabbath! *

TWO PARABLES OF THE KINGDOM

18 'What is the kingdom of God like?' he continued.
19 'What shall I compare it with? It is like a mustard-seed which a man took and sowed in his garden; and it grew to be a tree and the birds came to roost among its branches.'

20 Again he said, 'What shall I compare the kingdom of
21 God with? It is like yeast which a woman took and mixed with half a hundredweight of flour till it was all leavened.'

✲ 18–19. The kingdom of God is like a hidden growing process which from a small seed results in a great tree. The imagery of the tree and birds roosting in the branches suggests that Jesus has in mind the coming into being of a greater Israel (the tree) which will include non-Jews (the birds). The imagery is used in this way in Ezek. 17: 22–3.

20–1. The kingdom of God is again compared to a mysterious hidden process coming to a head. ✲

ON TO JERUSALEM

22 He continued his journey through towns and villages,
23 teaching as he made his way towards Jerusalem. Someone asked him, 'Sir, are only a few to be saved?' His
24 answer was: 'Struggle to get in through the narrow door; for I tell you that many will try to enter and not be able.
25 'When once the master of the house has got up and locked the door, you may stand outside and knock, and say, "Sir, let us in!", but he will only answer, "I do not
26 know where you come from." Then you will begin to say, "We sat at table with you and you taught in our

streets." But he will repeat, "I tell you, I do not know 27
where you come from. Out of my sight, all of you, you
and your wicked ways!" There will be wailing and 28
grinding of teeth there, when you see Abraham, Isaac,
and Jacob, and all the prophets, in the kingdom of God,
and yourselves thrown out. From east and west people 29
will come, from north and south, for the feast in the
kingdom of God. Yes, and some who are now last will 30
be first, and some who are first will be last.'

At that time a number of Pharisees came to him and 31
said, 'You should leave this place and go on your way;
Herod is out to kill you.' He replied, 'Go and tell that 32
fox, "Listen: today and tomorrow I shall be casting out
devils and working cures; on the third day I reach my
goal." However, I must be on my way today and 33
tomorrow and the next day, because it is unthinkable for
a prophet to meet his death anywhere but in Jerusalem.

'O Jerusalem, Jerusalem, the city that murders the 34
prophets and stones the messengers sent to her! How
often have I longed to gather your children, as a hen
gathers her brood under her wings; but you would not
let me. Look, look! there is your temple, forsaken by 35
God. And I tell you, you shall never see me until the
time comes when you say, "Blessings on him who comes
in the name of the Lord!"'

* 22–4. Jesus seems to have regarded questions whether all,
many or only few are to be saved as not for man to answer.
For practical purposes, he seems to be saying, it is better to
assume that few will be saved, and it is never wise for men
to assume the contrary, certainly as far as they themselves
are concerned.

25-30. Once again there is an intimate relationship between men's reactions to Jesus now and the character of the judgement to come. The figure of the master of the house is very like the coming Son of Man in Luke 12: 8-10. If those addressed are, as seems likely, Jews, the point is that belonging to God's chosen race does not solve the issue of faith. Many who, in Jewish eyes, could never qualify as true believers will in the end turn out to have done so.

31-3. Some popular presentations of Jesus suggest that he had no views on the political issues of his day but the description of Herod as *that fox* hardly argues political unawareness!

The phrase 'after three days' is commonly used, in both Old and New Testaments, for 'in a short time'. It seems likely that Jesus regarded his journey to Jerusalem as a 'must' laid upon him by the Father. It is in Jerusalem, he is convinced, that the Father will bring his plan to a head.

it is unthinkable for a prophet indicates that Jesus was aware of himself as standing in the prophetic tradition.

34-5. Once again Jesus speaks in verse, using the dirge rhythm characteristic of Hebrew poetry. He uses Jerusalem as a symbol for Israel as a whole. Israel had brutally rejected God's overtures (compare the parable of the vineyard tenants, Luke 20: 9-16). Jesus sees himself as Israel's ingatherer, and therefore fulfilling the purpose of God in reuniting his scattered Israel. This is a frequent theme in the Old Testament.

Ironically the temple of the Jews has now become more theirs than God's! This blindness to what is happening means that they will not see what the mission of Jesus is about until they see that he has become the foundation-stone of the new temple. Verse 35 ends with a quotation from Ps. 118. This was a psalm frequently in Jesus' mind, to judge from his use of the chief corner-stone idea. ✻

THE MAN WITH DROPSY

One Sabbath he went to have a meal in the house of a **14**
leading Pharisee; and they were watching him closely.
There, in front of him, was a man suffering from dropsy. 2
Jesus asked the lawyers and the Pharisees: 'Is it permitted 3
to cure people on the Sabbath or not?' They said nothing. 4
So he took the man, cured him, and sent him away.
Then he turned to them and said, 'If one of you has a 5
donkey or an ox and it falls into a well, will he hesitate to
haul it up on the Sabbath day?' To this they could find 6
no reply.

* 5. The phrase Jesus seems to have used most frequently in
this context is 'donkey or ox' (see 13: 15). Some manuscripts have 'son' instead of *donkey*. 'Son' and 'ox' appear
together in the Old Testament Law about working on the
Sabbath day (Deut. 5: 14). *

PARABLES ABOUT WEDDING AND DINNER PARTIES

When he noticed how the guests were trying to secure 7
the places of honour, he spoke to them in a parable:
'When you are asked by someone to a wedding-feast, 8
do not sit down in the place of honour. It may be that
some person more distinguished than yourself has been
invited; and the host will come and say to you, "Give 9
this man your seat." Then you will look foolish as you
begin to take the lowest place. No, when you receive an 10
invitation, go and sit down in the lowest place, so that
when your host comes he will say, "Come up higher,
my friend." Then all your fellow-guests will see the

11 respect in which you are held. For everyone who exalts himself will be humbled; and whoever humbles himself will be exalted.'

12   Then he said to his host, 'When you give a lunch or dinner party, do not invite your friends, your brothers or other relations, or your rich neighbours; they will only

13 ask you back again and so you will be repaid. But when you give a party, ask the poor, the crippled, the lame,

14 and the blind; and so find happiness. For they have no means of repaying you; but you will be repaid on the day when good men rise from the dead.'

15   One of the company, after hearing all this, said to him, 'Happy the man who shall sit at the feast in the kingdom

16 of God!' Jesus answered, 'A man was giving a big

17 dinner party and had sent out many invitations. At dinner-time he sent his servant with a message for his

18 guests, "Please come, everything is now ready." They began one and all to excuse themselves. The first said, "I have bought a piece of land, and I must go and look

19 over it; please accept my apologies." The second said, "I have bought five yoke of oxen, and I am on my way

20 to try them out; please accept my apologies." The next said, "I have just got married and for that reason I

21 cannot come." When the servant came back he reported this to his master. The master of the house was angry and said to him, "Go out quickly into the streets and alleys of the town, and bring me in the poor, the crippled, the

22 blind, and the lame." The servant said, "Sir, your orders

23 have been carried out and there is still room." The master replied, "Go out on to the highways and along the hedgerows and make them come in; I want my house to

be full. I tell you that not one of those who were invited 24
shall taste my banquet.'''

* 7–11. So many of the parables of Jesus which use the
imagery of banquets are concerned with the meaning of his
mission and discipleship that it is likely these parables are
about the same things. Jesus, and his disciples after him, are
summoned to a way of self-effacement. Honour and prestige
are not things they may seek for themselves.

12–14. The picture of a meal for *the poor, the crippled, the
lame, and the blind* reminds one of the mission of Jesus as he
outlined it, according to Luke, in the synagogue at Nazareth
(4: 18–19). In an ironic way the Pharisaic host is invited to
see that (in inviting Jesus) he has done what Jesus in his
mission does: seeks out the poor, etc. And to have treated
Jesus in this way will matter a great deal *on the day*.

15–24. Another allegorical parable about the mission of
Jesus, indicating how much Jesus was aware of being under
the Father's directives. God is summoning Israel to the
messianic banquet, and in Jesus (the *servant* of verse 17) proclaims it ready. The Israel of the day allows all kinds of self-
regarding considerations to prevent it seeing that this is in
fact happening. Jesus may have had in mind the reactions of
would-be disciples like those in Luke 9: 59–62. When rejected
by the Israel of his time Jesus, at the prompting of the Father,
issues the same summons to the outcasts of Israel. Israel is
excluding itself from its own festival. *

THE COST OF DISCIPLESHIP

Once when great crowds were accompanying him, he 25
turned to them and said: 'If anyone comes to me and 26
does not hate his father and mother, wife and children,
brothers and sisters, even his own life, he cannot be a
disciple of mine. No one who does not carry his cross and 27

28 come with me can be a disciple of mine. Would any of
you think of building a tower without first sitting down
and calculating the cost, to see whether he could afford
29 to finish it? Otherwise, if he has laid its foundation and
then is not able to complete it, all the onlookers will
30 laugh at him. "There is the man", they will say, "who
31 started to build and could not finish." Or what king will
march to battle against another king, without first sitting
down to consider whether with ten thousand men he can
face an enemy coming to meet him with twenty thousand?
32 If he cannot, then, long before the enemy approaches, he
33 sends envoys, and asks for terms. So also none of you
can be a disciple of mine without taking leave of all his
possessions.

34   'Salt is a good thing; but if salt itself becomes tasteless,
35 what will you use to season it? It is useless either on the
land or on the dung-heap: it can only be thrown away.
If you have ears to hear with, hear.'

✳ 26. God's summons makes serious demands. Discipleship
of Jesus is more than journeying about with a favourite
teacher. The link between Jesus and his disciples is of such a
kind that they share a common task and a common destiny.
There are a number of passages in the Old Testament where
'love' and *hate* are used in such a way as to make it clear that
hate means not 'to be hostile to' but 'to love less' (e.g. Deut.
21: 15: 'If a man have two wives, the one beloved, and the
other hated'). Discipleship means putting the closest family
ties in the context of the demands of Jesus.

    27. On discipleship as cross-bearing see note on Luke 9: 23.
    28–33. God is inviting all, through the activity of Jesus, to
enter the kingdom, but it is an invitation that ought not to be
casually accepted. It requires something like the careful

costing of a building scheme or preparations for a military operation. Discipleship of Jesus is not acting on impulse but carefully thought-out commitment.

34–5. It is that kind of devotion which will enable God to use the new community as seasoning in the world. ✻

PARABLES ABOUT LOSING AND FINDING

Another time, the tax-gatherers and other bad characters **15** were all crowding in to listen to him; and the Pharisees 2 and the doctors of the law began grumbling among them-selves: 'This fellow', they said, 'welcomes sinners and eats with them.' He answered them with this parable: 3 'If one of you has a hundred sheep and loses one of them, 4 does he not leave the ninety-nine in the open pasture and go after the missing one until he has found it? How 5 delighted he is then! He lifts it on to his shoulders, and 6 home he goes to call his friends and neighbours together. "Rejoice with me!" he cries. "I have found my lost sheep." In the same way, I tell you, there will be greater 7 joy in heaven over one sinner who repents than over ninety-nine righteous people who do not need to repent.

'Or again, if a woman has ten silver pieces and loses 8 one of them, does she not light the lamp, sweep out the house, and look in every corner till she has found it? And when she has, she calls her friends and neighbours 9 together, and says, "Rejoice with me! I have found the piece that I lost." In the same way, I tell you, there is joy 10 among the angels of God over one sinner who repents.'

Again he said: 'There was once a man who had two 11 sons; and the younger said to his father, "Father, give 12 me my share of the property." So he divided his estate

13 between them. A few days later the younger son turned the whole of his share into cash and left home for a distant country, where he squandered it in reckless living.
14 He had spent it all, when a severe famine fell upon that
15 country and he began to feel the pinch. So he went and attached himself to one of the local landowners, who sent
16 him on to his farm to mind the pigs. He would have been glad to fill his belly with the pods that the pigs were
17 eating; and no one gave him anything. Then he came to his senses and said, "How many of my father's paid servants have more food than they can eat, and here am
18 I, starving to death! I will set off and go to my father, and say to him, 'Father, I have sinned, against God and
19 against you; I am no longer fit to be called your son;
20 treat me as one of your paid servants.'" So he set out for his father's house. But while he was still a long way off his father saw him, and his heart went out to him. He ran to meet him, flung his arms round him, and kissed
21 him. The son said, "Father, I have sinned, against God and against you; I am no longer fit to be called your son."
22 But the father said to his servants, "Quick! fetch a robe, my best one, and put it on him; put a ring on his finger
23 and shoes on his feet. Bring the fatted calf and kill it,
24 and let us have a feast to celebrate the day. For this son of mine was dead and has come back to life; he was lost and is found." And the festivities began.

25 'Now the elder son was out on the farm; and on his way back, as he approached the house, he heard music
26 and dancing. He called one of the servants and asked
27 what it meant. The servant told him, "Your brother has come home, and your father has killed the fatted calf

because he has him back safe and sound." But he was 28
angry and refused to go in. His father came out and
pleaded with him; but he retorted, "You know how I 29
have slaved for you all these years; I never once disobeyed
your orders; and you never gave me so much as a kid,
for a feast with my friends. But now that this son of yours 30
turns up, after running through your money with his
women, you kill the fatted calf for him." "My boy," 31
said the father, "you are always with me, and everything
I have is yours. How could we help celebrating this 32
happy day? Your brother here was dead and has come
back to life, was lost and is found.'"

✻ Luke now begins a long section, chapters 15–19, in which
it becomes evident that Jesus saw his mission as carrying out
God's summons to Israel in the Old Testament to care for the
outcast and underprivileged.

1–7. It is probable that this parable is an indirect allusion to
a significant feature of the mission of Jesus: his association with
tax-gatherers and other bad characters. Jesus makes the same ironic
allusion to the *righteous people who do not need to repent* as in
5: 32 where, in answer to the complaint that he was eating
'with tax-gatherers and sinners' he replied: 'I have not come
to invite virtuous people, but to call sinners to repentance.'
For indications that Jesus saw his role as that of a shepherd
see 12: 32 ('Have no fear, little flock').

8–10. Or again the mission of Jesus is a demonstration of
the thoroughness with which God pursues his plan to save.
This searching love is given classic illustration in the next
parable.

11–32. This parable about a father and two sons is an
allegorical presentation of the significance of the mission of
Jesus. It reminds one of the other parable about two sons in
Matt. 21: 28 ff. The father's going out to the repentant son

points to Jesus' friendship for the socially outcast, people like tax-gatherers and harlots. The repentant son's career is in fact described in such a way as to suggest the *tax-gatherers and other bad characters* about whom we read in 15: 1.

The role of the elder son in the parable throws light on the attitude of Jesus to the Israel of his day. The elder brother seems to stand for Israel—concerned for itself and, in the case of the Pharisees, self-righteous. The elder son's catalogue of his virtues reads like the list the Pharisee gives of *his* virtues in the parable of the Pharisee and the tax-gatherer in Luke 18: 11–12. This self-regard, Jesus implies, is preventing Israel from seeing what is happening in his own day. God is summoning Israel to recognize the Gentiles as equals (*Your brother here*, verse 32) and to receive them gladly when they make a response. In the mission of Jesus both attitudes are being shown. ✳

THE DISHONEST BAILIFF

16 He said to his disciples, 'There was a rich man who had a bailiff, and he received complaints that this man was
2 squandering the property. So he sent for him, and said, "What is this that I hear? Produce your accounts, for
3 you cannot be manager here any longer." The bailiff said to himself, "What am I to do now that my employer is dismissing me? I am not strong enough to dig, and too
4 proud to beg. I know what I must do, to make sure that, when I have to leave, there will be people to give
5 me house and home." He summoned his master's debtors one by one. To the first he said, "How much do you
6 owe my master?" He replied, "A thousand gallons of olive oil." He said, "Here is your account. Sit down and
7 make it five hundred; and be quick about it." Then he said to another, "And you, how much do you owe?"

He said, "A thousand bushels of wheat", and was told, "Take your account and make it eight hundred." And 8 the master applauded the dishonest bailiff for acting so astutely. For the worldly are more astute than the other-worldly in dealing with their own kind.

'So I say to you, use your worldly wealth to win 9 friends for yourselves, so that when money is a thing of the past you may be received into an eternal home.

⁎ 1–8. This is a difficult parable to interpret. The tone is ironical throughout and this must be kept in mind. The context still seems to be God's way with man as hinted at in the mission of Jesus. God's summons to Israel through Jesus makes an emergency situation, a day of reckoning. The bailiff is quick enough to see what to do in the situation, and ready to take reckless action. Jesus constantly commended astuteness of this kind. One thinks of the Syro-Phoenician woman in Mark (7: 24–30) or of the blessing on the publicans and harlots who go into the kingdom of God before the Pharisees whose self-regard makes them too cautious (Matt. 21: 31). God is utterly ready to forgive, as the parable of the two sons has just shown, but this involves our ready forgiveness of others, and happy is the man who can produce evidence that this is what he has done! The story of the bailiff is the exact reverse of the rich man in 12: 16–21 who ended up 'a pauper in the sight of God'.

9. Again a saying which may have Israel in mind. Israel as a privileged people can be said to have *worldly wealth*. It would be sensible to use it to win friends from among those they have neglected, the Gentiles and the outcast. Such generosity would pay good dividends at the Judgement! ⁎

TRUE WEALTH

10 'The man who can be trusted in little things can be trusted also in great; and the man who is dishonest in little things
11 is dishonest also in great things. If, then, you have not proved trustworthy with the wealth of this world, who
12 will trust you with the wealth that is real? And if you have proved untrustworthy with what belongs to another, who will give you what is your own?

13   'No servant can be the slave of two masters; for either he will hate the first and love the second, or he will be devoted to the first and think nothing of the second. You cannot serve God and Money.'

14   The Pharisees, who loved money, heard all this and
15 scoffed at him. He said to them, 'You are the people who impress your fellow-men with your righteousness; but God sees through you; for what sets itself up to be admired by men is detestable in the sight of God.

16   'Until John, it was the Law and the prophets: since then, there is the good news of the kingdom of God, and everyone forces his way in.

17   'It is easier for heaven and earth to come to an end than for one dot or stroke of the Law to lose its force.

18   'A man who divorces his wife and marries another commits adultery; and anyone who marries a woman divorced from her husband commits adultery.

* 10–12. Jesus again uses the imagery of wealth to speak to disciples about forgiveness. If the disciples have not proved their worth, by forgiving in an unrighteous world, how unfitted they are for the wealth of God's forgiveness!

13–15. To the general statement in verse 13 that discipleship

means single-minded devotion Luke has added verses 14–15
which bring in the Pharisees as the audience.

16. An important saying which allows us to see the mission
of Jesus through his eyes. For him it was the beginning of a
new era, that of *the good news of the kingdom of God*. Those who
are quick to see this, people like the dishonest bailiff in verses
1–12, are forceful, even ruthless, about gaining entrance to
something of inestimable value.

17. In view of what has just preceded it, and of what
follows, this saying is best understood as a further example of
the irony of Jesus, and should have an exclamation mark. *One
dot or stroke* translates a Greek word which probably referred
to the ornamentation which scribes added to Hebrew letters.
So unbending is the legalism and literalism of the scribes that
Jesus can picture the universe being destroyed in some great
cataclysm, and the scribes still at work embroidering the
Scriptures! The legalistic mind never changes!

18. This, curiously, is the only reference in Luke to Jesus'
teaching on divorce. It does not seem to have been a subject
which particularly interested the evangelist. The saying that
he reproduces here shows Jesus not accepting the permission
for divorce granted by the law (Deut. 24: 1–4) if a husband
finds 'some unseemly thing' in his wife. He saw divorce as a
breach of an indissoluble oneness in marriage between man
and woman, and remarriage after divorce was therefore an
unwarrantable interference with this basic relationship. ✶

THE RICH MAN AND LAZARUS

'There was once a rich man, who dressed in purple and 19
the finest linen, and feasted in great magnificence every
day. At his gate, covered with sores, lay a poor man 20
named Lazarus, who would have been glad to satisfy his 21
hunger with the scraps from the rich man's table. Even
the dogs used to come and lick his sores. One day the 22

poor man died and was carried away by the angels to be
with Abraham. The rich man also died and was buried,
23 and in Hades, where he was in torment, he looked up; and
there, far away, was Abraham with Lazarus close beside
24 him. "Abraham, my father," he called out, "take pity
on me! Send Lazarus to dip the tip of his finger in water,
25 to cool my tongue, for I am in agony in this fire." But
Abraham said, "Remember, my child, that all the good
things fell to you while you were alive, and all the bad
to Lazarus; now he has his consolation here and it is you
26 who are in agony. But that is not all: there is a great
chasm fixed between us; no one from our side who wants
to reach you can cross it, and none may pass from your
27 side to us." "Then, father," he replied, "will you send
28 him to my father's house, where I have five brothers, to
warn them, so that they too may not come to this place
29 of torment?" But Abraham said, "They have Moses
30 and the prophets; let them listen to them." "No, father
Abraham," he replied, "but if someone from the dead
31 visits them, they will repent." Abraham answered, "If
they do not listen to Moses and the prophets they will pay
no heed even if someone should rise from the dead.'"

* Another parable of the folly of accumulating the wrong
kind of wealth. To be wrapped up in oneself, as the rich man
has been, means that one becomes blind to the real issues of the
day. One starts asking for a sign from heaven (verses 27–8)
although the real signs have been there all along (verses 30–1).

21. Lazarus is a name meaning 'God is help'. Very probably
he is an allegorical representation either of the ideal disciple
who, as one of the poor (Luke 6: 20) attains the kingdom,
or of Jesus himself. Even if Jesus is raised by God, this does
not mean that faith in him will therefore be easy. John 11

may be among other things a dramatization of the end of this parable to make this point. Lazarus *is* raised but the problem of faith remains. The Jews do not believe! *

TEACHING TO DISCIPLES

He said to his disciples, 'Causes of stumbling are bound to **17** arise; but woe betide the man through whom they come. It would be better for him to be thrown into the sea with 2 a millstone round his neck than to cause one of these little ones to stumble. Keep watch on yourselves. 3

'If your brother wrongs you, rebuke him; and if he repents, forgive him. Even if he wrongs you seven times 4 in a day and comes back to you seven times saying, "I am sorry", you are to forgive him.'

The apostles said to the Lord, 'Increase our faith'; and 5, 6 the Lord replied, 'If you had faith no bigger even than a mustard-seed, you could say to this sycamore-tree, "Be rooted up and replanted in the sea"; and it would at once obey you.

'Suppose one of you has a servant ploughing or mind- 7 ing sheep. When he comes back from the fields, will the master say, "Come along at once and sit down"? Will 8 he not rather say, "Prepare my supper, buckle your belt, and then wait on me while I have my meal; you can have yours afterwards"? Is he grateful to the servant for 9 carrying out his orders? So with you: when you have 10 carried out all your orders, you should say, "We are servants and deserve no credit; we have only done our duty."'

* 1–2. It is not easy to see what the original context of this saying was. Other versions of it come in Mark 9: 42 and

Matt. 18: 6–7. The way the saying has been transmitted in the tradition suggests that sayings of Jesus about children were confused with sayings about disciples, because he often called the latter 'children'.

The unsophisticated intuition and unaffectedness of children led Jesus to see in them the pattern of true discipleship. Hence the crime of putting anything in their way.

4. Forgiveness is endless.

5–6. Faith brings about the seemingly impossible—like endless forgiveness.

7–10. Discipleship is an entire, not a partial, commitment. As Paul eventually found, there can be no 'glorying' for the disciple ('What room then is left for human pride?', Rom. 3: 27). *

TEN LEPERS

11 In the course of his journey to Jerusalem he was travelling
12 through the borderlands of Samaria and Galilee. As he
   was entering a village he was met by ten men with
13 leprosy. They stood some way off and called out to him,
14 'Jesus, Master, take pity on us.' When he saw them he
   said, 'Go and show yourselves to the priests'; and while
15 they were on their way, they were made clean. One of
   them, finding himself cured, turned back praising God
16 aloud. He threw himself down at Jesus's feet and thanked
17 him. And he was a Samaritan. At this Jesus said: 'Were
   not all ten cleansed? The other nine, where are they?
18 Could none be found to come back and give praise to
19 God except this foreigner?' And he said to the man,
   'Stand up and go on your way; your faith has cured you.'

* This story of Jesus healing leprosy may have been based on an incident like that already recorded in Luke 5: 12–16. Be that as it may, it is clear that Luke presents this narrative as a

symbol that outcasts like Samaritans are readier to detect the significance of Jesus' mission than his own people, the Jews. ✻

THE DAY OF THE SON OF MAN

The Pharisees asked him, ' When will the kingdom of God 20 come?' He said, 'You cannot tell by observation when the kingdom of God comes. There will be no saying, "Look, 21 here it is!" or "there it is!"'; for in fact the kingdom of God is among you.'

He said to the disciples, 'The time will come when you 22 will long to see one of the days of the Son of Man, but you will not see it. They will say to you, "Look! There!" 23 and "Look! Here!" Do not go running off in pursuit. For like the lightning-flash that lights up the earth from 24 end to end, will the Son of Man be when his day comes. But first he must endure much suffering and be repudiated 25 by this generation.

'As things were in Noah's days, so will they be in the 26 days of the Son of Man. They ate and drank and married, 27 until the day that Noah went into the ark and the flood came and made an end of them all. As things were in 28 Lot's days, also: they ate and drank; they bought and sold; they planted and built; but the day that Lot went 29 out from Sodom, it rained fire and sulphur from heaven and made an end of them all—it will be like that on the 30 day when the Son of Man is revealed.

'On that day the man who is on the roof and his 31 belongings in the house must not come down to pick them up; he, too, who is in the fields must not go back. Remember Lot's wife. Whoever seeks to save his life will 32,33 lose it; and whoever loses it will save it, and live.

34   'I tell you, on that night there will be two men in one
35 bed: one will be taken, the other left. There will be two
    women together grinding corn: one will be taken, the
37 other left.' When they heard this they asked, 'Where,
    Lord?' He said, 'Where the corpse is, there the vultures
    will gather.'

☀ 20–1. The Pharisees' question amounts to a request for a
'sign from heaven' (see 11: 16). But the kingdom does not
come in a form which anyone can recognize in a superficial
effortless way. It is never that kind of indisputable fact.
There is the same note of irony in Jesus' reply as in his words
on a similar subject in 12: 56. If they knew how to look, the
signs they are looking for are certainly there. The kingdom is
among them—Jesus himself!

22–30. The manner in which God's kingdom comes does
not change. It never imposes itself willy-nilly. As the
kingdom comes in Jesus, so it will come in the *Son of Man*.
Then, as now, seeing it is a matter of a sudden unexpected
recognition.

25. Luke comes nearest of all the evangelists to drawing the
special attention of the reader to the mission of Jesus as one of
suffering and humiliation.

31–3. The final coming of the Son of Man will be a matter
of inescapable decision. No postponement of that decision
will be possible.

34–5. The day of the Son of Man inevitably involves
judgement and this means separation. Some manuscripts add
a verse 36 making the same point: 'two men in the fields: one
will be taken, the other left'.

37. Jesus repeats the point he made in verses 20–1. The
coming of the 'Son of Man' is not of the kind which can be
observed beforehand. The thing to do is to be like vultures
who are extraordinarily far-sighted and quick in their
recognition of the presence of food. ☀

ON PRAYER

He spoke to them in a parable to show that they should **18**
keep on praying and never lose heart: 'There was once a ₂
judge who cared nothing for God or man, and in the ₃
same town there was a widow who constantly came
before him demanding justice against her opponent. For ₄
a long time he refused; but in the end he said to himself,
"True, I care nothing for God or man; but this widow is ₅
so great a nuisance that I will see her righted before she
wears me out with her persistence."' The Lord said, 'You ₆
hear what the unjust judge says; and will not God vindi- ₇
cate his chosen, who cry out to him day and night, while
he listens patiently to them? I tell you, he will vindicate ₈
them soon enough. But when the Son of Man comes,
will he find faith on earth?'

And here is another parable that he told. It was aimed ₉
at those who were sure of their own goodness and looked
down on everyone else. 'Two men went up to the temple ₁₀
to pray, one a Pharisee and the other a tax-gatherer. The ₁₁
Pharisee stood up and prayed thus: "I thank thee, O
God, that I am not like the rest of men, greedy, dishonest,
adulterous; or, for that matter, like this tax-gatherer. I ₁₂
fast twice a week; I pay tithes on all that I get." But the ₁₃
other kept his distance and would not even raise his eyes
to heaven, but beat upon his breast, saying, "O God,
have mercy on me, sinner that I am." It was this man, I ₁₄
tell you, and not the other, who went home acquitted
of his sins. For everyone who exalts himself will be
humbled; and whoever humbles himself will be exalted.'

* 1-8. Luke intends the reader to link this parable with the preceding section. The prayer of the disciples 'Thy kingdom come' is a persistent one, continually to be prayed in the confidence that God will never cease to be the one who answers prayer. Jesus then wonders how long such a faith can hold out.

9-14. A parable directed against a certain type of self-conscious and self-righteous Pharisaism. True discipleship is to be marked by a realistic humility. *

QUALIFICATIONS FOR THE KINGDOM

15 They even brought babies for him to touch; but when
16 the disciples saw them they scolded them for it. But Jesus called for the children and said, 'Let the little ones come to me; do not try to stop them; for the kingdom of God
17 belongs to such as these. I tell you that whoever does not accept the kingdom of God like a child will never enter it.'
18   A man of the ruling class put this question to him:
19 'Good Master, what must I do to win eternal life?' Jesus said to him, 'Why do you call me good? No one is
20 good except God alone. You know the commandments: "Do not commit adultery; do not murder; do not steal; do not give false evidence; honour your father and
21 mother."' The man answered, 'I have kept all these since
22 I was a boy.' On hearing this Jesus said, 'There is still one thing lacking: sell everything you have and distribute to the poor, and you will have riches in heaven; and come,
23 follow me.' At these words his heart sank; for he was a
24 very rich man. When Jesus saw it he said, 'How hard
25 it is for the wealthy to enter the kingdom of God! It is easier for a camel to go through the eye of a needle than
26 for a rich man to enter the kingdom of God.' Those who

heard asked, 'Then who can be saved?' He answered, 27 'What is impossible for men is possible for God.'

Peter said, 'Here are we who gave up our belongings 28 to become your followers.' Jesus said, 'I tell you this: 29 there is no one who has given up home, or wife, brothers, parents, or children, for the sake of the kingdom of God, who will not be repaid many times over in this age, and 30 in the age to come have eternal life.'

✳ 15–17. There is a feeling for children noticeable in the teaching and manner of Jesus not found elsewhere in the New Testament nor among the early Fathers of the Church. God's kingdom comes in such a way that the qualities required for recognizing and entering it are the kind of openness, unsophisticated insight and unselfconsciousness that one sees best in little children.

18–19. Matthew alters the form of the question (Matt. 19: 17) apparently because it worried him that Jesus should hesitate to allow himself to be called good. The reply of Jesus given here (and in Mark 10: 18) indicates that Jesus was warning against the thoughtless casual use of words like *good*. Only God is perfectly *good*, and no one, not even Jesus himself, is to be called *good* in a way which forgets that fact. In an ironical way Jesus is asking the man to consider whether in calling him *good* he really believes himself to be confronted with God!

22–3. In this particular instance Jesus obviously thought discipleship must involve renunciation of possessions. Matthew (19: 21) turns the reply of Jesus into a general rule of perfection for all those who wish to follow Jesus.

24–7. Wealth makes it almost impossible to become a genuine disciple of Jesus. Zacchaeus (Luke 19: 1–10) was 'very rich' but it is only when he has given half his possessions to charity that he is told that salvation has come to his house.

28–30. There is reward, but it comes to those who do not seek one! ✳

169

Challenge to Jerusalem

APPROACHING JERUSALEM

31 HE TOOK the Twelve aside and said, 'We are now going up to Jerusalem; and all that was written by 32 the prophets will come true for the Son of Man. He will be handed over to the foreign power. He will be mocked, 33 maltreated, and spat upon. They will flog him and kill 34 him. And on the third day he will rise again.' But they understood nothing of all this; they did not grasp what he was talking about; its meaning was concealed from them.

35 As he approached Jericho a blind man sat at the road- 36 side begging. Hearing a crowd going past, he asked what 37 was happening. They told him, 'Jesus of Nazareth is 38 passing by.' Then he shouted out, 'Jesus, Son of David, 39 have pity on me.' The people in front told him sharply to hold his tongue; but he called out all the more, 'Son of 40 David, have pity on me.' Jesus stopped and ordered the man to be brought to him. When he came up he asked 41 him, 'What do you want me to do for you?' 'Sir, I 42 want my sight back', he answered. Jesus said to him, 43 'Have back your sight; your faith has cured you.' He recovered his sight instantly; and he followed Jesus, praising God. And all the people gave praise to God for what they had seen.

✳ 31-4. A third prediction of the humiliations and subse-quent glory of the *Son of Man*. He is bound to suffer the same treatment as Old Testament prophets, like (it seems) Jeremiah or the 'servant' in Isaiah.

35–43. The 'blindness' of the disciples who could not see the meaning of Jesus' words is followed by the episode of a blind beggar who is given his sight by Jesus and 'follows' him (as a disciple?). ✻

ZACCHAEUS

Entering Jericho he made his way through the city. **19**
There was a man there named Zacchaeus; he was 2
superintendent of taxes and very rich. He was eager to 3
see what Jesus looked like; but, being a little man, he
could not see him for the crowd. So he ran on ahead 4
and climbed a sycamore-tree in order to see him, for he
was to pass that way. When Jesus came to the place, he 5
looked up and said, 'Zacchaeus, be quick and come down;
I must come and stay with you today.' He climbed down 6
as fast as he could and welcomed him gladly. At this 7
there was a general murmur of disapproval. 'He has
gone in', they said, 'to be the guest of a sinner.' But 8
Zacchaeus stood there and said to the Lord, 'Here and
now, sir, I give half my possessions to charity; and if I
have cheated anyone, I am ready to repay him four times
over.' Jesus said to him, 'Salvation has come to this house 9
today!—for this man too is a son of Abraham, and the 10
Son of Man has come to seek and save what is lost.'

✻ 5. The language of Jesus is strong: *I* must *come and stay with you today*. It looks as if there was here the kind of interior prompting which led Jesus to take the situation as one of the Father's 'musts' for him.

7–10. This whole incident, found only in Luke, turns out to be a reproduction in miniature of the meaning of the mission of Jesus, and it seems that Jesus himself saw it that way. Here in Jesus is the coming of one who obeys the Old Testament summons to care for the oppressed and the outsiders. Zacchaeus' response to this, giving away half his wealth, points to the self-giving of true discipleship (compare the rich ruler in 18: 18-23). The whole incident is a pointer to the coming, in the *Son of Man*, of *salvation* to the *house* (of Israel —Zacchaeus is *a son of Abraham*). ✳

THE PARABLE OF THE POUNDS

11 While they were listening to this, he went on to tell them a parable, because he was now close to Jerusalem and they thought the reign of God might dawn at any mo-
12 ment. He said, 'A man of noble birth went on a long journey abroad, to be appointed king and then return.
13 But first he called ten of his servants and gave them a pound each, saying, "Trade with this while I am away."
14 His fellow-citizens hated him, and they sent a delegation on his heels to say, "We do not want this man as our
15 king." However, back he came as king, and sent for the servants to whom he had given the money, to see what
16 profit each had made. The first came and said, "Your
17 pound, sir, has made ten more." "Well done," he replied; "you are a good servant. You have shown yourself trustworthy in a very small matter, and you shall have
18 charge of ten cities." The second came and said, "Your
19 pound, sir, has made five more"; and he also was told,
20 "You too, take charge of five cities." The third came and said, "Here is your pound, sir; I kept it put away in
21 a handkerchief. I was afraid of you, because you are a hard man: you draw out what you never put in and
22 reap what you did not sow." "You rascal!" he replied; "I will judge you by your own words. You knew, did

you, that I am a hard man, that I draw out what I never
put in, and reap what I did not sow? Then why did you 23
not put my money on deposit, and I could have claimed
it with interest when I came back?" Turning to his 24
attendants he said, "Take the pound from him and give it
to the man with ten." "But, sir," they replied, "he has 25
ten already." "I tell you," he went on, "the man who 26
has will always be given more; but the man who has not
will forfeit even what he has. But as for those enemies of 27
mine who did not want me for their king, bring them
here and slaughter them in my presence.'"

✷ A similar parable to this is found in Matt. 25: 14–30. We
have noted indications that Jesus saw his journey to Jerusalem
as the beginning of a procession to a royal throne where the
Father would crown him. Two meanings of the parable can
be detected in the version Luke gives here. Originally this
parable may have been, on the lips of Jesus, an allegory of his
whole mission, with particular reference to what he can see
coming in Jerusalem. His *fellow-citizens* (the Jews) are rejecting a *man of noble birth* (Jesus) who has been appointed
their king. By doing this they will bring destruction on
themselves. A second meaning is that the disciples must
hold on in loyalty and obedience, confident that their servant-
master will return as a crowned king. This is the meaning
suggested by the introductory comment in verse 11. The
final appearance of the kingdom of God had not come with the
death and resurrection of Jesus. The crowning of Jesus is still
to come. Meanwhile the disciples have the tasks which he has
allotted to them. The use by Jesus of illustrations from banking
(verse 23) or execution (verse 27) does not mean that his
teaching sanctions capitalism or killing of enemies! ✷

ASCENT TO JERUSALEM

28 With that Jesus went forward and began the ascent to
29 Jerusalem. As he approached Bethphage and Bethany at
30 the hill called Olivet, he sent two of the disciples with
these instructions: 'Go to the village opposite; as you
enter it you will find tethered there a colt which no one
31 has yet ridden. Untie it and bring it here. If anyone asks
why you are untying it, say, "Our Master needs it."'
32 The two went on their errand and found it as he had told
33 them; and while they were untying the colt, its owners
34 asked, 'Why are you untying that colt?' They answered,
35 'The Master needs it.' So they brought the colt to Jesus.

Then they threw their cloaks on the colt, for Jesus to
36 mount, and they carpeted the road with them as he went
37 on his way. And now, as he approached the descent
from the Mount of Olives, the whole company of his
disciples in their joy began to sing aloud the praises of
God for all the things they had seen:

38   'Blessings on him who comes as king in the name of
       the Lord!
    Peace in heaven, glory in highest heaven!'

39   Some Pharisees who were in the crowd said to him,
40 'Master, reprimand your disciples.' He answered, 'I tell
you, if my disciples keep silence the stones will shout
aloud.'

41,42   When he came in sight of the city, he wept over it and
said, 'If only you had known, on this great day, the way
that leads to peace! But no; it is hidden from your sight.
43 For a time will come upon you, when your enemies will

set up siege-works against you; they will encircle you and hem you in at every point; they will bring you to the ground, you and your children within your walls, and not leave you one stone standing on another, because you did not recognize God's moment when it came.' 44

Then he went into the temple and began driving out the traders, with these words: 'Scripture says, "My house shall be a house of prayer"; but you have made it a robbers' cave.' 45 46

Day by day he taught in the temple. And the chief priests and lawyers were bent on making an end of him, with the support of the leading citizens, but found they were helpless, because the people all hung upon his words. 47 48

* 28–35. Jesus deliberately planned his entry into Jerusalem. He made it into a royal procession of such a kind (and this the Pharisees saw clearly—verse 39) as to raise acutely the question: Is this Israel's Messiah? It is a particularly impressive example of the ambiguous manner of his mission, and of the irony thus inevitably produced. He *is* proclaimed king in the capital which will give him only a mock-coronation! As Matthew suggests (Matt. 21: 5), this episode may well have been a deliberate dramatization by Jesus of Zech. 9: 9: 'Rejoice greatly, O daughter of Zion; shout, O daughter of Jerusalem: behold, thy king cometh unto thee: he is just, and having salvation; lowly, and riding upon an ass, even upon a colt the foal of an ass.'

38. Luke's version of what the crowd shout out: *Peace in heaven, glory in highest heaven!* (compare Matthew's 'Hosanna in the heavens!', 21: 9) suggests that he wishes the reader to be reminded of the angels' song at the Nativity (2: 14).

40. Jesus is so intensely aware of what is really happening that he suggests men would have to be more insensitive than stone not to have some idea of what is taking place.

41–4. This lamentation over Jerusalem is in a form which suggests that in the original Aramaic Jesus spoke here in verse, showing the ironic play on words which is frequently noticeable in his teaching. Jerusalem (which might mean 'city of peace') cannot see when true peace comes! Jesus takes this as a 'sign' of the times (*God's moment*—verse 44) and sees the coming siege and destruction of Jerusalem (possibly by the Romans) as poetic justice—a symbol of God's judgement on lack of trust. The tears of Jesus are the tears of tragedy: his love for Jerusalem is in tension with his acceptance of its judgement.

45–6. According to Mark one of the charges brought against Jesus was that he had said: 'I will throw down this temple, made with human hands, and in three days I will build another, not made with hands' (Mark 14: 58), and this threat seems to have become one of the things popularly associated with Jesus. When he is on the cross the crowds shout at him 'you would pull the temple down, would you, and build it in three days?' (Mark 15: 29). It seems very probable that what has now become known as the 'cleansing' of the temple was originally some kind of messianic demonstration, a dramatized 'sign' of the presence of the new temple. Jesus did not literally destroy the temple but was the beginning of a new and spiritual temple which took the place of the old building of stone. The temple was destroyed by the Romans in A.D. 70. This may be the reason why the incident has become transformed in the tradition into a 'cleansing' where Jesus criticizes the traders for converting the temple into a market. John 2: 21–2 is a reminder to readers of his Gospel of the original meaning of the incident.

The *Scripture* referred to in verse 46 is Isa. 56: 7. ✳

FROM GOD OR FROM MEN?

One day, as he was teaching the people in the temple and **20**
telling them the good news, the priests and lawyers, and
the elders with them, came upon him and accosted him. 2
'Tell us', they said, 'by what authority you are acting
like this; who gave you this authority?' He answered
them, 'I have a question to ask you too: tell me, was the ³
baptism of John from God or from men?' This set them ⁴
arguing among themselves: 'If we say, "from God", he ⁵
will say, "Why did you not believe him?" And if we 6
say, "from men", the people will all stone us, for they are
convinced that John was a prophet.' So they replied that 7
they could not tell. And Jesus said to them, 'Neither will 8
I tell you by what authority I act.'

✻ 1–8. An extremely important passage revealing not only
how Jesus saw John the Baptist but also the way in which he
believed he must conduct his mission and deal with requests
to declare himself unambiguously. It is significant that when
asked to identify himself and show his credentials (verse 2) the
mind of Jesus immediately went back to John the Baptist. His
questioners are faced with the same decision as himself: was
John the Baptist just another prophetic revivalist or a 'sign
from heaven', to use their own term (Luke 11: 16)? Inability
to make up one's mind about John the Baptist meant even
greater inability to recognize Jesus. If they could not recognize the heralding of the kingdom in John, they certainly
would not see the presence of it in Jesus. To answer their
question for them would be a violation of the Father's
commission; he can only convey the meaning of himself by
parable, such as the one which follows. ✻

THE PARABLE OF THE VINE-GROWERS

9 He went on to tell the people this parable: 'A man planted a vineyard, let it out to vine-growers, and went abroad
10 for a long time. When the season came, he sent a servant to the tenants to collect from them his share of the produce; but the tenants thrashed him and sent him
11 away empty-handed. He tried again and sent a second servant; but he also was thrashed, outrageously treated,
12 and sent away empty-handed. He tried once more with
13 a third; this one too they wounded and flung out. Then the owner of the vineyard said, "What am I to do? I will send my own dear son; perhaps they will respect him."
14 But when the tenants saw him they talked it over together. "This is the heir," they said; "let us kill him so that the
15 property may come to us." So they flung him out of the vineyard and killed him. What then will the owner of
16 the vineyard do to them? He will come and put these tenants to death and let the vineyard to others.'

17 When they heard this, they said, 'God forbid!' But he looked straight at them and said, 'Then what does this text of Scripture mean: "The stone which the builders
18 rejected has become the main corner-stone"? Any man who falls on that stone will be dashed to pieces; and if it falls on a man he will be crushed by it.'

* This parable is an allegorical presentation of the meaning of Jesus' mission as he himself saw it. He uses the picture of Israel as God's vineyard which appears in Isa. 5: 1–7. Jesus sees God sending 'his servants the prophets' (Amos 3: 7) to an Israel which consistently refuses to accept them. He sees his own mission as a unique last summons which the Israel of his day will in the end reject. But this will not be the end of God's purpose to build an Israel. Jesus sees his mission resulting in the reconstitution of Israel so as to include the Gentiles.

17. *God forbid!* probably expresses the horror felt by Jewish listeners at the idea that Israel should include others than Jews. In reply, Jesus uses one of his persistent images: that of a new building, a new temple. Here he quotes from Ps. 118: 22, and thinks of himself as a rejected stone which mysteriously turns out to be *the main corner-stone* of a new house of Israel.

18. Where the stone is accepted, as for example by Peter's recognition at Caesarea Philippi, Jesus is seen to be the impregnable foundation of a new structure (Matt. 16: 18). ✳

TAXES TO CAESAR?

The lawyers and chief priests wanted to lay hands on him there and then, for they saw that this parable was aimed at them; but they were afraid of the people. So they watched their opportunity and sent secret agents in the guise of honest men, to seize upon some word of his as a pretext for handing him over to the authority and jurisdiction of the Governor. They put a question to him: 'Master,' they said, 'we know that what you speak and teach is sound; you pay deference to no one, but teach in all honesty the way of life that God requires. Are we or are we not permitted to pay taxes to the Roman Emperor?' He saw through their trick and said, 'Show me a silver piece. Whose head does it bear, and whose inscription?' 'Caesar's', they replied. 'Very well then,' he said, 'pay Caesar what is due to Caesar, and pay God what is due to God.' Thus their attempt to catch him out in public failed, and, astonished by his reply, they fell silent.

✻ Another example of the irony of Jesus. When asked whether it is right for Jews to pay the poll-tax levied by the Romans he pointed to the image (*head*) of Caesar stamped on the coins. It is right, he indicates, for the state to exact what has its stamp on it, but he implies that the state may not take for itself what has God's image stamped on it, and what that is his questioners must decide! Caesar has God's image stamped on him so even the things which seem to be Caesar's are really God's! ✻

WHAT HAPPENS AT THE RESURRECTION?

27 Then some Sadducees came forward. They are the people who deny that there is a resurrection. Their question was
28 this: 'Master, Moses laid it down for us that if there are brothers, and one dies leaving a wife but no child, then the next should marry the widow and carry on his
29 brother's family. Now, there were seven brothers: the
30 first took a wife and died childless; then the second married
31 her, then the third. In this way the seven of them died
32 leaving no children. Afterwards the woman also died.
33 At the resurrection whose wife is she to be, since all
34 seven had married her?' Jesus said to them, 'The men
35 and women of this world marry; but those who have been judged worthy of a place in the other world and of
36 the resurrection from the dead, do not marry, for they are not subject to death any longer. They are like angels; they are sons of God, because they share in the resurrection.
37 That the dead are raised to life again is shown by Moses himself in the story of the burning bush, when he calls the
38 Lord, "the God of Abraham, Isaac, and Jacob". God is not God of the dead but of the living; for him all are alive.'
39 At this some of the lawyers said, 'Well spoken, Master.'

For there was no further question that they ventured to 40
put to him.

* 27. *some Sadducees.* The Sadducees, like the Pharisees,
originated as a party within Judaism at the time of the
Maccabees (second century B.C.). Generally speaking, they
were an aristocratic and conservative element. Many Sadducees were dignitaries in the priesthood. They were funda-
mentalists in their interpretation of the Law, sticking to a
literal interpretation and rejecting the attempts of the Pharisees
to relate the Law to all aspects of life. They rejected also
the Pharisaic belief in resurrection. Politically they were
'collaborationists' willing, as a means of preserving Israel, to
collaborate with Rome.

28. This is a reference to what was called 'levirate' marriage
('levirate' because 'levir' is the Latin for brother-in-law)
described in Deut. 25: 5–10. For a number of reasons (the
chief of which was to keep the family name alive) it was
thought important for a man to have sons. If, therefore, he
died without having any his wife was expected to marry her
husband's brother and any sons born to them were regarded
as the sons of the first husband. In this way his name would
not be 'blotted out of Israel' (Deut. 25: 6).

34–6. The resurrection-life is not this life over again, but
a new existence of sonship to God, participating in his eternity.

37–8. The episode of Moses and *the burning bush* comes in
Exod. 3. Moses' way of addressing God is a reminder that
God will not cease to be the God he has disclosed himself to
be to those who have readily responded to his promptings. *

SON OF DAVID
LAWYERS AND A WIDOW

He said to them, 'How can they say that the Messiah is 41
son of David? For David himself says in the Book of 42
Psalms: "The Lord said to my Lord, 'Sit at my right

43,44 hand until I make your enemies your footstool.'" Thus David calls him "Lord"; how then can he be David's son?'

45   In the hearing of all the people Jesus said to his disciples:
46 'Beware of the lawyers who love to walk up and down in long robes, and have a great liking for respectful greetings in the street, the chief seats in our synagogues, and places
47 of honour at feasts. These are the men who eat up the property of widows, while they say long prayers for appearance' sake; and they will receive the severest sentence.'

21   He looked up and saw the rich people dropping their
2 gifts into the chest of the temple treasury; and he noticed
3 a poor widow putting in two tiny coins. 'I tell you this,' he said: 'this poor widow has given more than any of
4 them; for those others who have given had more than enough, but she, with less than enough, has given all she had to live on.'

✻ Yet another oblique and ironic comment of Jesus on a matter relating to his own identity. The Old Testament itself suggests that there is more to the Messiah than mere descent from David, who himself had called the Messiah his 'Lord'! How much of this 'more' are they prepared to see in Jesus?

42. Jesus shared the common belief that the Psalms were written by David; the quotation is from Ps. 110: 1.

45–7. A saying directed against religious humbug and exploitation by the educated of those less able to defend themselves.

21: 1–4. The reference to *widows* in 20: 47 has led Luke to use here an episode to illustrate a theme of the Gospel: how wealth gets in the way of true self-giving. ✻

THINGS TO COME

Some people were talking about the temple and the 5
fine stones and votive offerings with which it was
adorned. He said, 'These things which you are gazing 6
at—the time will come when not one stone of them will
be left upon another: all will be thrown down.' 'Master,' 7
they asked, 'when will it all come about? What will be
the sign when it is due to happen?'

He said, 'Take care that you are not misled. For many 8
will come claiming my name and saying, "I am he",
and, "The Day is upon us." Do not follow them. And 9
when you hear of wars and insurrections, do not fall into
a panic. These things are bound to happen first; but the
end does not follow immediately. Nation will make war 10
upon nation, kingdom upon kingdom; there will be 11
great earthquakes, and famines and plagues in many
places; in the sky terrors and great portents.

'But before all this happens they will set upon you and 12
persecute you. You will be brought before synagogues
and put in prison; you will be haled before kings and
governors for your allegiance to me. This will be your 13
opportunity to testify; so make up your minds not to 14
prepare your defence beforehand, because I myself will 15
give you power of utterance and a wisdom which no
opponent will be able to resist or refute. Even your 16
parents and brothers, your relations and friends, will
betray you. Some of you will be put to death; and you 17
will be hated by all for your allegiance to me. But not a 18
hair of your head shall be lost. By standing firm you will 19
win true life for yourselves.

20 'But when you see Jerusalem encircled by armies,
21 then you may be sure that her destruction is near. Then
those who are in Judaea must take to the hills; those who
are in the city itself must leave it, and those who are out
22 in the country must not enter; because this is the time of
retribution, when all that stands written is to be fulfilled.
23 Alas for women who are with child in those days, or have
children at the breast! For there will be great distress in
24 the land and a terrible judgement upon this people. They
will fall at the sword's point; they will be carried captive
into all countries; and Jerusalem will be trampled down
by foreigners until their day has run its course.

25 'Portents will appear in sun, moon, and stars. On
earth nations will stand helpless, not knowing which way
26 to turn from the roar and surge of the sea; men will faint
with terror at the thought of all that is coming upon the
27 world; for the celestial powers will be shaken. And
then they will see the Son of Man coming on a cloud
28 with great power and glory. When all this begins to
happen, stand upright and hold your heads high, because
your liberation is near.'

29 He told them this parable: 'Look at the fig-tree, or any
30 other tree. As soon as it buds, you can see for yourselves
31 that summer is near. In the same way when you see all
this happening, you may be sure that the kingdom of
God is near.

32 'I tell you this: the present generation will live to see
33 it all. Heaven and earth will pass away; my words will
never pass away.

34 'Keep a watch on yourselves; do not let your minds be
dulled by dissipation and drunkenness and worldly cares

so that the great Day closes upon you suddenly like a trap; 35 for that day will come on all men, wherever they are, the whole world over. Be on the alert, praying at all times 36 for strength to pass safely through all these imminent troubles and to stand in the presence of the Son of Man.'

His days were given to teaching in the temple; and 37 then he would leave the city and spend the night on the hill called Olivet. And in the early morning the people 38 flocked to listen to him in the temple.

* The difficulty of this section is that sayings of Jesus about the destruction of Jerusalem, which he could see coming, have been linked with words of his about the coming 'Day of the Son of Man'.

5–7. This is a prediction that the temple in Jerusalem will soon be destroyed. The signs that this is coming about are given in verses 20–4.

8–11. There will always be those who will say they know when the day is and will proclaim themselves Messiahs. For Jesus, a Messiah who openly names himself such is certainly bogus.

12–19. An important passage showing that in the mind of Jesus discipleship is bound to be similar to the pattern of his own ministry. We have already been told (12: 12) that the Holy Spirit will prompt disciples in emergency. Now, in a way that reminds one of the teaching of John's Gospel on the Holy Spirit, this is explained as the means whereby Jesus himself will give power to his followers.

20–4. In the manner and style of an Old Testament prophet Jesus predicts the siege and destruction of Jerusalem.

25–8. After startling convulsions in the natural world there will be seen the Son of Man in triumph. The reference is to Dan. 7: 13. We cannot be certain that when Jesus said *they will see the Son of Man coming* he meant that they would see him returning to earth. Most people have assumed that this was his meaning in this and similar sayings, for example in his reply to the high priest: 'you will see the Son of Man seated on the right hand of God and coming with the clouds of heaven' (Mark 14: 62). By *coming on a cloud* Jesus may have meant being taken in a cloud of glory into God's presence. This is certainly what is described in Dan. 7: 13 where the Son of Man comes 'with the clouds of heaven' to be crowned with glory by 'the ancient of days' (God). It is possible to argue that this *coming* into God's presence was mistakenly thought by the early Church to be a *coming* back to earth, a 'second coming' of Christ. Those who take the view that Jesus meant a *coming* to God regard the beginning of the kingdom of Christ as the moment when he takes his place 'on the throne at the right hand of God' (at the ascension).

Others have thought that the beginning of Christ's kingdom would be when he came back to reign on earth. The interpretation of these sayings is always a subject for discussion among New Testament scholars.

29–31. The signs of the presence of the kingdom are always of such a kind that men ought to recognize them (compare 12: 54–6).

32–3. The Judaism of Jesus' day had inherited the belief that the Law was eternal ('the Law that endureth for ever', Baruch 4: 1). This saying is another indication that Jesus saw the Israel of the Old Testament being shaped afresh in his own ministry; the new Law of the new Israel was being proclaimed if men had ears to hear it.

After verse 38 some manuscripts have here the story of 'the woman detected in adultery'. Most manuscripts include this in John's Gospel (John 7: 53 — 8: 11). This story is very probably one of the detached units of genuine material about Jesus which some early Christians were anxious to get into one Gospel or another. ✶

The Final Conflict

22: 1 — 24: 53

✡ In his record of the passion of Jesus Luke has drawn to some extent upon his source, Mark, but has shown himself much freer than Matthew in drawing upon other material at his disposal. There is a recognizable Lucan interpretation of the crucifixion which is important for an understanding of the author's second volume, Acts. For Luke the death of Jesus is, among other things, the perfect and unique martyrdom. In Acts it is a martyr, like Stephen, who is the typical imitator of Christ. Luke's account of the passion gives no cry of desertion from the cross as in Mark and Matthew. Jesus does not pray for himself but for others, and he dies nobly (23: 47). There is some resemblance to Greek tragedy with the chorus of weeping women who lament for Jesus (23: 27, 48). Luke comes nearest of all the Gospels to touching on the emotional character of the scene.

There is a marked similarity between the accounts of the passion in Luke and John. Both Gospels, for example, speak of the role of Satan in the betrayal of Jesus; there are conversations at the last supper where also Peter's denial is foretold; Jesus has the initiative and is not the powerless victim of the other Gospels; both evangelists insist more than Mark and Matthew on the animosity of the Jews and Pilate's efforts to save Jesus; and in the Calvary scene both stress the dignity and serenity of Jesus.

THE LORD'S PASSOVER

NOW THE FESTIVAL of Unleavened Bread, known as **22**
Passover, was approaching, and the chief priests and 2
the doctors of the law were trying to devise some means

of doing away with him; for they were afraid of the people.

3 Then Satan entered into Judas Iscariot, who was one
4 of the Twelve; and Judas went to the chief priests and officers of the temple police to discuss ways and means of
5 putting Jesus into their power. They were greatly pleased
6 and undertook to pay him a sum of money. He agreed, and began to look out for an opportunity to betray him to them without collecting a crowd.

7 Then came the day of Unleavened Bread, on which the
8 Passover victim had to be slaughtered, and Jesus sent Peter and John with these instructions: 'Go and prepare
9 for our Passover supper.' 'Where would you like us to
10 make the preparations?' they asked. He replied, 'As soon as you set foot in the city a man will meet you carrying a jar of water. Follow him into the house that
11 he enters and give this message to the householder: "The Master says, 'Where is the room in which I may eat the
12 Passover with my disciples?'" He will show you a large room upstairs all set out: make the preparations there.'
13 They went and found everything as he had said. So they prepared for Passover.

14 When the time came he took his place at table, and the
15 apostles with him; and he said to them, 'How I have longed to eat this Passover with you before my death!
16 For I tell you, never again shall I eat it until the time when it finds its fulfilment in the kingdom of God.'

17 Then he took a cup, and after giving thanks he said,
18 'Take this and share it among yourselves; for I tell you, from this moment I shall drink from the fruit of the vine no more until the time when the kingdom

of God comes.' And he took bread, gave thanks, and 19
broke it; and he gave it to them, with the words: 'This
is my body.'

'But mark this—my betrayer is here, his hand with 21
mine on the table. For the Son of Man is going his 22
appointed way; but alas for that man by whom he is
betrayed!' At this they began to ask among themselves 23
which of them it could possibly be who was to do this
thing.

✻ What was the 'last supper' and when did it take place?
These are less easy questions to answer than the precision of
the Christian Church's calendar and liturgy suggest. The
uncertainty springs from what seems to be a discrepancy between the timing of the last supper and crucifixion as
given (*a*) in the Synoptic Gospels, and (*b*) in John.

In Mark (and Matthew who follows him) the last supper
was the Passover meal ('they prepared for Passover',
Mark 14: 16; Matt. 26: 19). This would mean that it was eaten
early on what was, in the Jewish calendar, 15 Nisan. Since
the Jewish day began at sunset, this would be in what we
would call early evening, and on this same day (i.e. before the
next sunset) the arrest, trial and crucifixion of Jesus took
place.

In John everything takes place a day earlier. The crucifixion
was on the day before Passover, 14 Nisan ('It was now early
morning, and the Jews themselves stayed outside the headquarters to avoid defilement, so that they could eat the
Passover meal', John 18: 28; 'It was the eve of Passover',
19: 14). The last supper, according to this scheme, must
have been held at the beginning of 14 Nisan, and was not
apparently a Passover meal.

If the last supper was not a Passover meal it has been
suggested that it must have been one of the ritual fellowship
meals common then (and now) in Jewish domestic tradition.

Jesus gave this customary meal a special association on this occasion by his cryptic allusions to the significance of the bread and the wine. If the 'shorter text' is what Luke wrote, this may well be what he thought about the meal. This 'shorter text' is that printed in the N.E.B. (Luke 22: 17–19). At the end of Luke 22: 19 some manuscripts give a longer version of what Jesus said on this occasion. After '"This is my body"' it continues: '"which is given for you; do this as a memorial of me". In the same way he took the cup after supper, and said, "This cup, poured out for you, is the new covenant sealed by my blood".' On this 'longer text' see the note on 22: 17–19.

Recent research seems to favour the interpretation of the last supper as a Passover meal. In that case Mark and Matthew give us the real time-sequence, and John has moved things back because of his 'Lamb of God' theme; in John Jesus is crucified just at the time when the Passover lambs were being killed. Compare Paul's 'our Passover has begun; the sacrifice is offered—Christ himself', I Cor. 5: 7.

This interpretation would be strengthened if we accepted the view, outlined in the note on 9: 3, that Jesus pictured his whole mission as a Passover, a going-over of the significant moments in the history of old Israel, culminating in a last pilgrimage to Jerusalem for the festival itself.

3–6. Luke, like the author of John, explicitly ascribes the action of Judas to Satan (see John 13: 27). We cannot be certain what the motive for the betrayal of Jesus by Judas was. Perhaps Judas, like another of Jesus' disciples, Simon (Luke 6: 15), was sympathetic to the Zealot movement, which wanted to use force against the Romans. Jesus was not a Zealot, but he may have attracted Zealots like Judas. Judas apparently became convinced that Jesus' failure to turn his mission into a political force was not just a mistake of tactics but so great a menace to 'progressive' forces in Judaea that he must denounce his master.

7–13. Jesus deliberately arranged for this Passover meal in

the same way as he had previously ordered his entry into
Jerusalem. The careful planning indicates the central importance of the occasion for Jesus.

15. This Passover meal was, it seems, so urgent a 'must' at
this stage of the mission that Jesus feared that destiny might
rob him of it.

17-19. In the shorter version of Luke the emphasis is on the
occasion as a toast to the future, an anticipation when they
will all sit at the messianic banquet. The longer version is
possibly due to a desire to bring Luke's Gospel into line with
the accounts in Matthew and Mark and the earliest account of
the last supper in 1 Cor. 11: 23-5.

21-2. Notice the oblique manner of Jesus in indicating the
traitor. Jesus indicates that the *Son of Man* must continue
along the way to which he has committed himself, and this
seems to be the way of Israel outlined in the servant poems of
Isaiah. Yet Judas' action remains free and responsible but it
will have consequences he cannot realize. He is caught up in a
tragedy greater than he could conceive. ✳

LAST DISCOURSE

Then a jealous dispute broke out: who among them 24
should rank highest? But he said, 'In the world, kings 25
lord it over their subjects; and those in authority are
called their country's "Benefactors". Not so with you: 26
on the contrary, the highest among you must bear
himself like the youngest, the chief of you like a servant.
For who is greater—the one who sits at table or the ser- 27
vant who waits on him? Surely the one who sits at
table. Yet here am I among you like a servant.

'You are the men who have stood firmly by me in my 28
times of trial; and now I vest in you the kingship which 29
my Father vested in me; you shall eat and drink at my 30

table in my kingdom and sit on thrones as judges of the twelve tribes of Israel.

31 'Simon, Simon, take heed: Satan has been given leave
32 to sift all of you like wheat; but for you I have prayed that your faith may not fail; and when you have come to
33 yourself, you must lend strength to your brothers.' 'Lord,' he replied, 'I am ready to go with you to prison and
34 death.' Jesus said, 'I tell you, Peter, the cock will not crow tonight until you have three times over denied that you know me.'

35 He said to them, 'When I sent you out barefoot without purse or pack, were you ever short of anything?'
36 'No', they answered. 'It is different now,' he said; 'whoever has a purse had better take it with him, and his pack too; and if he has no sword, let him sell his cloak to buy
37 one. For Scripture says, "And he was counted among the outlaws", and these words, I tell you, must find fulfilment in me; indeed, all that is written of me is being
38 fulfilled.' 'Look, Lord,' they said, 'we have two swords here.' 'Enough, enough!' he replied.

✻ Yet another similarity to John's Gospel is this discourse which Luke places at the last supper. The Jewish Passover meal included a long discourse answering the question 'What do you mean by this service?' (see Exod. 12: 26). Jesus explains the meaning of his 'Passover' ministry, and the main theme, as in John, is the mission to be the 'servant' (see John 13: 1–17).

28–30. The whole mission of Jesus has been a trial of his obedience and willingness to act on the 'signs' the Father has been giving. This is also a feature of the mission of his disciples. He and they form one royal community to whom the power of judgement will be assigned.

31–4. Satan will test disciples like Peter just as he tested Jesus.

35–8. A saying full of the characteristic ironies of Jesus. The test of faith begins now! Disciples of the outcast one are likely to encounter henceforth hostility and lack of assistance where previously they had been welcomed. Jesus ironically suggests that they will need a good sword to defend them now! This ironic saying of Jesus is taken literally (a common feature of John's Gospel) and Jesus abruptly says 'That's enough of that'.

37. This is the only place in the Gospels where Jesus is shown making explicit reference to the suffering-servant theme in the book of Isaiah. Here he refers to Isa. 53: 12. ✴

ON THE MOUNT OF OLIVES

Then he went out and made his way as usual to the Mount 39 of Olives, accompanied by the disciples. When he 40 reached the place he said to them, 'Pray that you may be spared the hour of testing.' He himself withdrew from 41 them about a stone's throw, knelt down, and began to pray: 'Father, if it be thy will, take this cup away from 42 me. Yet not my will but thine be done.'

And now there appeared to him an angel from heaven 43 bringing him strength, and in anguish of spirit he prayed 44 the more urgently; and his sweat was like clots of blood falling to the ground.

When he rose from prayer and came to the disciples 45 he found them asleep, worn out by grief. 'Why are you 46 sleeping?' he said. 'Rise and pray that you may be spared the test.'

✴ 42. *cup* is a frequent image in the Old Testament for suffering which has to be endured as medicine has to be drunk.

See, for example, Ezek. 23: 33: 'Thou shalt be filled with drunkenness and sorrow, with the cup of astonishment and desolation.'

43–4. These verses are omitted by some manuscripts but since it is not difficult to see the motives which led to their removal they are probably genuine. Jesus felt real fear and anxiety as he faced death not only as the end but as a symbol of sin's alienation from God, and as he faced also what he saw as the power of Satan.

45. Only Luke attempts to exonerate the disciples by suggesting, curiously, that their tiredness was due to grief! *

THE ARREST OF JESUS

47 While he was still speaking a crowd appeared with the man called Judas, one of the Twelve, at their head. He
48 came up to Jesus to kiss him; but Jesus said, 'Judas, would you betray the Son of Man with a kiss?'

49 When his followers saw what was coming, they said,
50 'Lord, shall we use our swords?' And one of them struck at the High Priest's servant, cutting off his right ear.
51 But Jesus answered, 'Let them have their way.' Then he touched the man's ear and healed him.

52 Turning to the chief priests, the officers of the temple police, and the elders, who had come to seize him, he said, 'Do you take me for a bandit, that you have come
53 out with swords and cudgels to arrest me? Day after day, when I was in the temple with you, you kept your hands off me. But this is your moment—the hour when darkness reigns.'

54 Then they arrested him and led him away. They brought him to the High Priest's house, and Peter
55 followed at a distance. They lit a fire in the middle of the

courtyard and sat round it, and Peter sat among them.
A serving-maid who saw him sitting in the firelight 56
stared at him and said, 'This man was with him too.' But 57
he denied it: 'Woman,' he said, 'I do not know him.'
A little later someone else noticed him and said, 'You 58
also are one of them.' But Peter said to him, 'No, I am
not.' About an hour passed and another spoke more 59
strongly still: 'Of course this fellow was with him. He
must have been; he is a Galilean.' But Peter said, 'Man, 60
I do not know what you are talking about.' At that
moment, while he was still speaking, a cock crew; and 61
the Lord turned and looked straight at Peter. And Peter
remembered the Lord's words, 'Tonight before the cock
crows you will disown me three times.'

The men who were guarding Jesus mocked at him. 63
They beat him, they blindfolded him, and they kept ask- 64
ing him, 'Now, prophet, who hit you? Tell us that.'
And so they went on heaping insults upon him. 65

✻ 47–8. Peculiar to Luke is the suggestion that Judas did not
actually *kiss* Jesus (Mark and Matthew both say that he did)
and that Jesus explicitly named himself *the Son of Man* (in
Mark Jesus makes no reply to Judas, and this is more characteristic of him; in Matthew he says, 'Friend, do what you are here
to do', 26: 50). The form of the saying about the *kiss* in
verse 48 may reflect the fact that by the time the Gospel was
written the kiss had become a significant symbol of Christian
love, and the evangelist finds it distasteful to think of Judas
using it. And for reasons discussed earlier it is not likely that
Jesus used the title *Son of Man* in this explicit way.

49–51. The disciples, in a simple-minded way, assume that
Jesus' saying in verse 36 means that ordinary swords can save
the situation, but once again Jesus dismisses the idea. The

healing of the man's ear is a touch peculiar to Luke, and is one of the details used in arguing that the writer was a doctor.

52–3. There are two features here that remind one of John's Gospel: (1) darkness as an image for what is hostile to Jesus, and (2) the idea that his ministry is punctuated by moments which sharply focus the contest between God and evil. This saying shows that these Johannine features have a basis in Jesus' imaginative thought.

54–65. Daringly, and in a mood similar to that of John, the evangelist puts here a 'trial' of Peter which forms an ironic sub-plot to the main drama which is to come. Peter claims not to be what he is; Jesus does not claim to be what in fact he is. The soldiers play blind-man's buff with Christ, but to the reader of his Gospel the scene is prophetic in a way the soldiers could not realize. ✳

THE TRIALS OF JESUS

66 When day broke, the elders of the nation, chief priests, and doctors of the law assembled, and he was brought
67 before their Council. 'Tell us,' they said, 'are you the Messiah?' 'If I tell you,' he replied, 'you will not believe
68,69 me; and if I ask questions, you will not answer. But from now on, the Son of Man will be seated at the right hand
70 of Almighty God.' 'You are the Son of God, then?' they
71 all said, and he replied, 'It is you who say I am.' They said, 'Need we call further witnesses? We have heard it ourselves from his own lips.'

23 With that the whole assembly rose, and they brought
2 him before Pilate. They opened the case against him by saying, 'We found this man subverting our nation, opposing the payment of taxes to Caesar, and claiming to
3 be Messiah, a king.' Pilate asked him, 'Are you the king

of the Jews?' He replied, 'The words are yours.' Pilate 4
then said to the chief priests and the crowd, 'I find no
case for this man to answer.' But they insisted: 'His 5
teaching is causing disaffection among the people all
through Judaea. It started from Galilee and has spread
as far as this city.'

When Pilate heard this, he asked if the man was a 6
Galilean, and on learning that he belonged to Herod's 7
jurisdiction he remitted the case to him, for Herod was
also in Jerusalem at that time. When Herod saw Jesus he 8
was greatly pleased; having heard about him, he had long
been wanting to see him, and had been hoping to see
some miracle performed by him. He questioned him 9
at some length without getting any reply; but the chief 10
priests and lawyers appeared and pressed the case against
him vigorously. Then Herod and his troops treated him 11
with contempt and ridicule, and sent him back to Pilate
dressed in a gorgeous robe. That same day Herod and 12
Pilate became friends: till then there had been a standing
feud between them.

Pilate now called together the chief priests, councillors, 13
and people, and said to them, 'You brought this man 14
before me on a charge of subversion. But, as you see,
I have myself examined him in your presence and found
nothing in him to support your charges. No more did 15
Herod, for he has referred him back to us. Clearly he has
done nothing to deserve death. I therefore propose to 16
let him off with a flogging.' But there was a general 18
outcry, 'Away with him! Give us Barabbas.' (This man 19
had been put in prison for a rising that had taken place
in the city, and for murder.) Pilate addressed them again, 20

197

21 in his desire to release Jesus, but they shouted back,
22 'Crucify him, crucify him!' For the third time he spoke
to them: 'Why, what wrong has he done? I have not
found him guilty of any capital offence. I will therefore
23 let him off with a flogging.' But they insisted on their
demand, shouting that Jesus should be crucified. Their
24 shouts prevailed and Pilate decided that they should have
25 their way. He released the man they asked for, the man
who had been put in prison for insurrection and murder,
and gave Jesus up to their will.

* 66–71. Jesus brought before the 'Supreme Court' of the
Jews (the Sanhedrin) was asked to identify himself as the
Messiah. Characteristically he replied in the cryptic manner
he adopted in this kind of situation. Instead of labelling himself one way or the other he spoke of a coming triumph of the
Son of Man in such a manner that it was assumed by his
interrogators that he was admitting Messiahship.

23: 1–5. The charges against Jesus brought by the Jews to
Pilate were that he was politically and socially subversive.
Again Jesus left the question whether he were a king or not to
his accusers.

6–12. This episode occurs only in Luke and some scholars
have doubted whether this trial before Herod ever took place.
It is important to notice that when in Acts 4: 25–8 Luke
mentions the trials before Herod and Pilate, it is in the context
of a quotation from Ps. 2: 1–2:

> The kings of the earth set themselves,
> And the rulers take counsel together,
> Against the Lord, and against his anointed.

Luke has certainly included the incident as part of his attempt
to remove responsibility for the death of Jesus from the Roman
authorities.

13–25. The threefold plea of Pilate ((*a*) verses 14–16;

(*b*) verse 20; (*c*) verse 22) for the release of Jesus reads, again, like a device of Luke's to exonerate the Roman governor.

Some manuscripts insert a further verse after 16 'At festival time he was obliged to release one person for them'. This reference to the practice of releasing a prisoner at the festival is probably an attempt to make clear to the reader what would otherwise be a rather abrupt reference to Barabbas. ✳

THE CRUCIFIXION

As they led him away to execution they seized upon a 26 man called Simon, from Cyrene, on his way in from the country, put the cross on his back, and made him walk behind Jesus carrying it.

Great numbers of people followed, many women 27 among them, who mourned and lamented over him. Jesus turned to them and said, 'Daughters of Jerusalem, 28 do not weep for me; no, weep for yourselves and your children. For the days are surely coming when they will 29 say, "Happy are the barren, the wombs that never bore a child, the breasts that never fed one." Then they 30 will start saying to the mountains, "Fall on us", and to the hills, "Cover us." For if these things are done 31 when the wood is green, what will happen when it is dry?'

There were two others with him, criminals who were 32 being led away to execution; and when they reached the 33 place called The Skull, they crucified him there, and the criminals with him, one on his right and the other on his left. Jesus said, 'Father, forgive them; they do not know 34 what they are doing.'

They divided his clothes among them by casting lots.

35 The people stood looking on, and their rulers jeered at him: 'He saved others: now let him save himself, if this
36 is God's Anointed, his Chosen.' The soldiers joined in the mockery and came forward offering him their sour wine.
37 'If you are the king of the Jews,' they said, 'save yourself.'
38 There was an inscription above his head which ran: 'This is the king of the Jews.'

39   One of the criminals who hung there with him taunted him: 'Are not you the Messiah? Save yourself, and us.'
40 But the other answered sharply, 'Have you no fear of
41 God? You are under the same sentence as he. For us it is plain justice; we are paying the price for our misdeeds; but
42 this man has done nothing wrong.' And he said, 'Jesus,
43 remember me when you come to your throne.' He answered, 'I tell you this: today you shall be with me in Paradise.'

44   By now it was about midday and there came a darkness over the whole land, which lasted until three in the
45 afternoon; the sun was in eclipse. And the curtain of the
46 temple was torn in two. Then Jesus gave a loud cry and said, 'Father, into thy hands I commit my spirit'; and
47 with these words he died. The centurion saw it all, and gave praise to God. 'Beyond all doubt', he said, 'this man was innocent.'

48   The crowd who had assembled for the spectacle, when they saw what had happened, went home beating their breasts.

✱ 26. Luke alone goes out of his way to present Simon as a cross-bearer behind Jesus. He is a picture of the ideal disciple who has been summoned to take up his cross 'day after day' (Luke 9: 23). In the Synoptic Gospels there is no attempt to

picture Jesus as a hero carrying his own cross (compare John
19: 17).

27–31. This chorus of weeping women reminds one of
Greek tragedy. Compare also the lamentation over Jerusalem
in Zech. 12: 11–14. Once again Jesus predicts the coming
destruction of Jerusalem (cf. 19: 43–4; 21: 20–4).

31. The meaning of this saying may be that if the Romans
do this to one who has merely enacted kingship in a cryptic
manner, it is all the more likely that a worse fate awaits those
who openly and explicitly proclaim themselves, such as, for
instance, the Zealots.

34. This verse is omitted in some manuscripts but Luke
clearly intended Stephen's forgiveness of his executioners (see
Acts 7: 60) to be an example of the true disciple who imitates
his master, and therefore it is most probably genuine. Unfortunately, we have then to assume that some copyist dropped
the saying because he wished to insist on Jewish responsibility
and could not believe that the Jews were forgivable, even by
Jesus! The second half of verse 34 is practically a quotation
from Ps. 22: 18:

> They part my garments among them,
> And upon my vesture do they cast lots

which may have influenced the detail here. It was the custom
to crucify naked.

37–8. Luke mentions the inscription over the cross as part
of the mockery of Jesus. He has drawn sufficient attention in
the body of his Gospel to the real kingship of Jesus and the
salvation he brings to enable his readers to appreciate the
irony of the situation. Jesus was never more *king* and saviour
than on the cross!

39–43. Both Luke and John show a tendency to see the
crucifixion scene symbolically. John sees in the mother and
the beloved disciple types of the old Israel and the new Israel
(the Church). Here there may be something like the allegorical
treatment of the prodigal son and the elder brother in the Lucan

parable (15: 11–32). The penitence of the criminal, like that of the prodigal son, enables him to see the presence of salvation.

43. Like John, Luke takes the view that Jesus entered into his glory on crucifixion (John 13: 31).

44–8. A paragraph of events to which Luke gives symbolic importance. There may have been a sudden mysterious *darkness* at the time. Luke ascribes it to an *eclipse*, apparently forgetting that such an event would be impossible at the Passover season which was held at full-moon. But the darkness reminds one of Jesus' saying at the arrest: 'this is your moment—the hour when darkness reigns' (Luke 22: 53). The darkness is of the seeming defeat of Jesus by the forces of evil. The bright light of the men in 'dazzling garments' (24: 4) is the sign that the darkness has been overcome. There may have been some mysterious tearing of *the curtain* which hung in front of the most holy part of the temple (the 'holy of holies'). But Luke, like Matthew and Mark, uses the idea as a symbol of the creation of a new Israel which would include non-Jews. As Paul put it, in Christ 'there is no such thing as Jew and Greek' (Gal. 3: 28).

46–7. The cry from the cross in Luke is not one of desertion as in Mark (15: 34) but a perfect example of 'Thy will be done'. Luke sees in the death of Jesus the example of how a Christian should die. And so just as Jesus commits himself to God with the words *Father, into thy hands I commit my spirit*, Stephen, at his death, commits himself to Jesus in similar words: 'Lord Jesus, receive my spirit' (Acts 7: 59). Again, only in Luke is there mention of a general lamentation for Jesus on the part of the crowd. ✶

BURIAL AND RESURRECTION

49 His friends had all been standing at a distance; the women who had accompanied him from Galilee stood with them and watched it all.

50   Now there was a man called Joseph, a member of the

Council, a good, upright man, who had dissented from 51
their policy and the action they had taken. He came from
the Jewish town of Arimathaea, and he was one who
looked forward to the kingdom of God. This man now 52
approached Pilate and asked for the body of Jesus.
Taking it down from the cross, he wrapped it in a linen 53
sheet, and laid it in a tomb cut out of the rock, in which
no one had been laid before. It was Friday, and the 54
Sabbath was about to begin.

The women who had accompanied him from Galilee 55
followed; they took note of the tomb and observed how
his body was laid. Then they went home and prepared 56
spices and perfumes; and on the Sabbath they rested in
obedience to the commandment. But on the Sunday **24**
morning very early they came to the tomb bringing the
spices they had prepared. Finding that the stone had been 2
rolled away from the tomb, they went inside; but the 3
body was not to be found. While they stood utterly at a 4
loss, all of a sudden two men in dazzling garments were
at their side. They were terrified, and stood with eyes 5
cast down, but the men said, 'Why search among the
dead for one who lives? Remember what he told you 6
while he was still in Galilee, about the Son of Man: how 7
he must be given up into the power of sinful men and be
crucified, and must rise again on the third day.' Then 8
they recalled his words and, returning from the tomb, 9
they reported all this to the Eleven and all the others.

The women were Mary of Magdala, Joanna, and Mary 10
the mother of James, and they, with the other women,
told the apostles. But the story appeared to them to be 11
nonsense, and they would not believe them.

* 49. The synoptic evangelists all speak of the relatives and friends of Jesus watching from a distance. This is more likely to have been what happened, rather than John's account of the mother and the beloved disciple standing at the foot of the cross. The Romans did not permit bystanders at the actual place of execution. John's account is influenced by his symbolic aim. The mother (old Israel) is handed over to the care of the 'beloved disciple' (who represents the new Israel of the Christian Church).

53. Luke shares with John the special note that the tomb was one *in which no one had been laid before* (see John 19: 41).

24: 4. In Mark the women see a 'youth...wearing a white robe' (Mark 16: 5). In Matthew it is 'an angel of the Lord'. Luke has two men in *dazzling garments* and they appear again in his account of the ascension in Acts 1: 10.

11. After this verse some manuscripts have 'Peter, however, got up and ran to the tomb, and, peering in, saw the wrappings and nothing more; and he went home amazed at what had happened'. This has some similarity with John 20: 3–10 and verse 24 of this chapter seems to be referring back to it. It is not easy to see why it should have been omitted. *

THE WAY TO EMMAUS

13 That same day two of them were on their way to a village called Emmaus, which lay about seven miles from
14 Jerusalem, and they were talking together about all these
15 happenings. As they talked and discussed it with one another, Jesus himself came up and walked along with
16 them; but something held their eyes from seeing who it
17 was. He asked them, 'What is it you are debating as you
18 walk?' They halted, their faces full of gloom, and one, called Cleopas, answered, 'Are you the only person staying in Jerusalem not to know what has happened there in the

last few days?' 'What do you mean?' he said. 'All this 19
about Jesus of Nazareth,' they replied, 'a prophet powerful in speech and action before God and the whole
people; how our chief priests and rulers handed him over 20
to be sentenced to death, and crucified him. But we had 21
been hoping that he was the man to liberate Israel. What
is more, this is the third day since it happened, and now 22
some women of our company have astounded us: they
went early to the tomb, but failed to find his body, and 23
returned with a story that they had seen a vision of angels
who told them he was alive. So some of our people 24
went to the tomb and found things just as the women had
said; but him they did not see.'

'How dull you are!' he answered. 'How slow to 25
believe all that the prophets said! Was the Messiah not 26
bound to suffer thus before entering upon his glory?'
Then he began with Moses and all the prophets, and 27
explained to them the passages which referred to himself
in every part of the scriptures.

By this time they had reached the village to which they 28
were going, and he made as if to continue his journey,
but they pressed him: 'Stay with us, for evening draws 29
on, and the day is almost over.' So he went in to stay
with them. And when he had sat down with them at 30
table, he took bread and said the blessing; he broke the
bread, and offered it to them. Then their eyes were 31
opened, and they recognized him; and he vanished from
their sight. They said to one another, 'Did we not feel 32
our hearts on fire as he talked with us on the road and
explained the scriptures to us?'

* A very important passage for understanding the significance of the resurrection of Christ in early Christian belief. The resurrection was a 'sign' to see, requiring that one's eyes should be properly opened (verse 16). The place of this disclosure was the breaking of the bread (verses 30–1). This association of the 'eucharist' and realization of the presence of the risen Lord is a feature also of John's Gospel. It may explain why so many of the stories of appearances of the risen Christ are associated with meals.

It was the resurrection which alone gave meaning to the whole mission of Jesus (verses 25–7). The 'Son of Man' had a way to go before entering his glory. He had to be obedient Israel. The early Christians were to insist on Jesus as the one who fulfilled scripture and the evidence is that they did this because Jesus had first done so himself. To realize the presence of Christ is to be aware of him as the illuminator of scripture (verse 32). *

APPEARANCES IN JERUSALEM

33 Without a moment's delay they set out and returned to Jerusalem. There they found that the Eleven and the rest
34 of the company had assembled, and were saying, 'It is
35 true: the Lord has risen; he has appeared to Simon.' Then they gave their account of the events of their journey and told how he had been recognized by them at the breaking of the bread.

36   As they were talking about all this, there he was,
37 standing among them. Startled and terrified, they thought
38 they were seeing a ghost. But he said, 'Why are you so perturbed? Why do questionings arise in your minds?
39 Look at my hands and feet. It is I myself. Touch me and see; no ghost has flesh and bones as you can see that I have.'
41 They were still unconvinced, still wondering, for it

seemed too good to be true. So he asked them, 'Have
you anything here to eat?' They offered him a piece of 42
fish they had cooked, which he took and ate before their 43
eyes.

And he said to them, 'This is what I meant by saying, 44
while I was still with you, that everything written about
me in the Law of Moses and in the prophets and psalms
was bound to be fulfilled.' Then he opened their minds 45
to understand the scriptures. 'This', he said, 'is what is 46
written: that the Messiah is to suffer death and to rise
from the dead on the third day, and that in his name 47
repentance bringing the forgiveness of sins is to be proclaimed to all nations. Begin from Jerusalem: it is you 48
who are the witnesses to all this. And mark this: I am 49
sending upon you my Father's promised gift; so stay here
in this city until you are armed with the power from
above.'

Then he led them out as far as Bethany, and blessed 50
them with uplifted hands; and in the act of blessing he 51
parted from them. And they returned to Jerusalem with 52
great joy, and spent all their time in the temple praising 53
God.

✻ In Luke the appearances of the risen Christ are all in or near
Jerusalem; in Matthew they happened in Galilee. John's
Gospel gives appearances both in Galilee and Jerusalem. The
reason for Luke's reference to appearances in Jerusalem may
be due to the intention which he had in mind for his second
volume. If the subject of his first book was the mission of
Jesus from Galilee to Jerusalem, the theme of his second work
was to be the mission of Jesus (shaped by the Spirit at work in
the Church) from Jerusalem to Rome.

36-49. This story, like the episode of doubting Thomas

in John 20: 19–29, aims at explaining belief in the risen Christ. Indeed there are verbal similarities between the two passages. As in John the suggestion made is that there is more to belief in the resurrection than physical seeing. Here even touching and seeing a physically risen Lord does not issue in belief. What is needed is the opening of their minds to understand the scriptures (verse 45). Perhaps the suggestion of the whole passage is that the normal place for full realization of the presence of the risen Christ is at the eucharistic assembly when scripture is expounded.

49. Luke, again because of the requirements of his two-volume work, distinguishes more sharply between resurrection, ascension and the giving of the Spirit. In John they are moments in one divine act of redemption.

50–3. The last picture of Christ in this Gospel is as the priest giving his blessing *with uplifted hands*. This is yet another link with John where Jesus is also pictured as a priest (compare the Letter to Hebrews).

51. Some manuscripts add 'and was carried up into heaven'. This may well be the original reading which was later omitted because at the beginning of Acts the ascension is an event which takes place forty days after the resurrection (Acts 1: 3).

52. Our last view of the disciples in this Gospel is of them worshipping in the Jewish temple. The tragedy of the breach with the synagogue was yet to come. This is to be one of the themes in Luke's second volume to which he expects his readers will now turn, and as they read Acts they will be reminded again and again of the main themes of this Gospel. ✻

✻ ✻ ✻ ✻ ✻ ✻ ✻ ✻ ✻ ✻ ✻ ✻ ✻

CONCLUSION

When we look back over his first volume, these are the points which Luke has made with special emphasis:

1. *Christianity as 'the way'*

Luke's characteristic expression for the Christian religion is 'The Way' ('the new way', Acts 9: 2; 'a way of salvation', Acts 16: 17; 'the way of the Lord', Acts 18: 25 are a few instances). 'The Way' as a title for Christianity is not found only in Luke's writings; it occurs in John's Gospel where Jesus himself says 'I am the way, I am the truth and I am life' (John 14: 6) and in the Letter to Hebrews where the author speaks of Jesus as 'the new, living way' (Heb. 10: 20). Nevertheless, it is a theme which Luke has specially emphasized in his two volumes. The Gospel of Luke and Acts are, in fact, two books on 'the way': the 'way of Christ' in the Gospel and the 'way of the Christian' in Acts. In the manner of John, Luke announces this theme in the prologue to his Gospel and then develops it in the main body of the work. John the Baptist is to prepare 'the way' (Luke 1: 76) of him who is to 'guide our feet into the way of peace' (Luke 1: 79).

Jesus is in Luke's Gospel essentially a journeying figure. It appears that Luke, again like John, wants the readers of his Gospel to see in the actual travelling of Jesus, especially the journey up to Jerusalem, which is heralded as a decisive event in Luke 9: 51, a symbol of the other event which is going on at the same time: the going up to God. The way up to Jerusalem (in obedience) is the way up to heaven (in ascension —Luke 9: 51 and 19: 28). It is therefore a way of salvation (Luke 1: 77), a new exodus of Israel from sin and death (see note on Luke 9: 31), a Passover celebrating Israel's freedom by enacting the journey from Egypt to the promised land. Luke uses the journeys of the apostles in Acts to make the point that Christians are those who follow in Christ's 'way', or rather that in Christians Christ, through the Spirit, is making another return journey to the Father. In the 'way of Christ' as it is presented in the Gospel Luke intends his Christian readers to see *their* way from baptism into Christ to ascension to Christ.

2. The 'sign of the Son of Man'

Only Luke of the synoptic evangelists explicitly describes the mission of Jesus as the sign of the Son of Man (Luke 11: 30). This is again a theme which he has already announced in the prologue to the Gospel: 'This child is destined to be a sign which men reject...and....Many in Israel will stand or fall because of him' (Luke 2: 34–5). A 'sign' is an ordinary happening which points beyond itself (for those who have the faith to see) to the presence of God. The 'sign' given to the shepherds is quite ordinary: 'you will find a baby lying all wrapped up, in a manger' (Luke 2: 12) but behind this they were able to hear the song of angels (Luke 2: 14). They both *saw* and *heard* (Luke 2: 20).

In his wanderings, in his call of the Twelve, in his symbolic feeding of the multitude, in his deliberately seeking the poor and outcast, in the dramatically staged entry into Jerusalem, in the 'cleansing of the temple' and the last supper, Jesus was deliberately pointing to the fulfilment of Israel's destiny in himself. He and the Twelve were the new wandering Israel, entering the royal capital for crowning ('now I vest in you the kingship which my Father vested in me', Luke 22: 29) and enacting the new covenant between God and Israel at the last supper. This use of symbolic action was characteristic of the Old Testament prophets and Luke presents Jesus as summing up all that was significant in the prophetic tradition. He is the new Elijah.

This 'way' of Jesus, because it was ambiguous (the ordinary being at the same time not so ordinary) was inevitably a 'stumbling-block' for some. The point of parables is seen by some, not by others; the 'signs' given in certain events are recognized by some but not by others. The way God worked in Christ was a way which at every point respected human freedom. The way Jesus spoke and acted was always of such a kind as to leave men free to pass their own judgement on him. Hence the place of irony in his method which we have noted in the commentary. The things he said and did always pointed to something else as well as their ordinary meaning. Jesus was well aware that he was expected to give proofs that would settle everything ("'Physician heal yourself!"... "do the same here in your own home town"', Luke 4: 23) but he saw the task given him by the Father that he should allow himself to be a sign rather than give proofs of his own. This meant that the meaning of the mission of Jesus could always be disputed; it was both 'sign' and 'stumbling-block' but 'happy is the man who does not find me a stumbling-block' (Luke 7: 23). Perhaps Jesus found the 'Son of Man' a term most apt to express the character of his mission because it could mean both something ordinary (a man, a human being) and something unusual (a people, Israel, what the book of Daniel calls the 'saints of the Most High'—Dan. 7: 22). Significantly, in the book of Daniel the Son of Man is both a figure of suffering and also one who is triumphantly crowned. As 'the saints of the Most High' the 'Son of Man' has suffered greatly from the 'horn' (Antiochus Epiphanes who tried to compel the Jews to conform to the Greek way of life) (Dan. 7: 21). But the 'Son of Man' is also crowned by the 'ancient of days' (God) (Dan. 7: 27). Jesus' use of 'Son of Man' could therefore mean, in one way, that his mission was 'as one of the prophets' and neither more nor less significant than that. But it could also mean (for those who were prepared to take it this way) that he was in some sense Israel, the Son of Man, destined to be crowned in glory.

3. *Lordship and discipleship*

By linking his Gospel with Acts Luke clearly intended his readers to see the unique relationship which exists between Jesus the risen, ascended and exalted Lord and the Christian disciple. In Acts the preaching and death of Stephen is presented in a way which recalls Jesus himself (see Acts 6: 8 — 8: 1), and the ministries of Peter (Acts chs. 2–12) and Paul (Acts, chs. 13–28) have basically the same pattern as that of their Lord. The life of Jesus for Luke is the pattern for Christians, and, as Acts shows, the Christian life is a matter of being moulded by the Spirit into conformity with Christ the model. The Gospel of Luke is about discipleship at the same time as it is about Jesus, just as Acts is about Jesus at the same time as it is about Christians. That is to say, in the Gospel the history of the mission of Jesus is presented to the reader in a way which indicates that the pattern of Jesus' life is the model for the Christian, and in Acts behind the sayings and actions of Christians there is the Lord Christ, whom the Holy Spirit shows to be not only the object of their faith but the very means of it. The narrative of the ministry of Jesus in the Gospel of Luke has been influenced by the belief about the relationship between 'Lord' and disciple as it appears in Acts. That is why in Luke 'Lord' as a title for Jesus is more prominent than in any other Gospel. In the call of Peter, for example (Luke 5: 1–11), Luke sees both an actual summons of Peter during Jesus' lifetime, and also the Lord summoning one of his key apostles to the task we see him performing in Acts 2–12.

In Luke's Gospel Jesus is the Christian's pattern of prayer, of service, of suffering and the Christian life in Acts means being shaped by the Holy Spirit into a likeness of Christ.

4. *The Spirit and Life*

The dominant impression remaining as we leave the Gospel of Luke is of a Christ conscious of being endowed by the Spirit for the particular task of presenting, in terms of his own personal obedience, service and suffering, the fulfilment of Israel's age-old vocation to walk in the way of the Lord. This is what he must do; what would result from it is the Father's secret. Jesus must go on confident that what the Father willed would be brought about. The Spirit worked in Jesus as he set about the work of giving glory to the Father. In Jesus, God's whole purpose in history had come to a head: to create a human community, a people, an Israel, whose relationship to God would be one of freedom and love. This is the meaning of the dramatic proclamation, 'The spirit of the Lord is upon me because he has anointed me' (Luke 4: 18) which Luke placed at the head of his account of the ministry of Jesus (Luke 4: 14–21). The first two chapters of the Gospel have been deliberately constructed as an Old Testament in miniature, showing the Holy Spirit at work preparing the setting for the work of Jesus who is himself to be the embodiment of Israel.

Acts is written in the conviction that the Holy Spirit who worked in Christ will not cease to work in his disciples. In the Gospel the Spirit comes with Christ, in Acts Christ comes with the Spirit. It is the one coming of the one God who always comes the same way—by 'signs'! Significantly the final words of Paul with which Luke leaves us at the end of Acts are a repetition (in the language of Isa. 6) of the warning which Christ himself gave: 'Take care, then, how you listen' (Luke 8: 18).

A NOTE ON FURTHER STUDY

The only satisfactory way of appreciating the distinctive qualities of Luke's Gospel in comparison with Matthew and Mark is to use a synopsis where these three Gospels are set out side by side. These Gospels are called 'synoptic' just because they lend themselves to this treatment. Good synopses based on the English text are *Gospel Parallels* (published by Nelson) and J. M. Thompson's *The Synoptic Gospels*. *Gospel Parallels* is so arranged that each Gospel can be read through continuously alongside parallel passages from the other two.

Two good first books on the Synoptic Gospels are J. H. Ropes, *The Synoptic Gospels* and C. H. Dodd, *About the Gospels* (now printed with his *The Coming of Christ*). For the literary problems in the study of the Gospels see Vincent Taylor, *The*

Gospels, a short introduction, and for the formation of the Gospel tradition E. Basil Redlich, *Form-Criticism*.

An excellent short book on Luke's Gospel is R. H. Fuller, *Luke's Witness to Jesus Christ* and a handy commentary, by G. B. Caird, is now available in The Pelican Gospel Commentaries. Perhaps the most stimulating large-scale commentary on the Synoptic Gospels remains that of C. G. Montefiore (*The Synoptic Gospels*, 2 volumes), written from a liberal Jewish point of view. For the relation of Luke's Gospel to Acts a good book is Henry J. Cadbury's *The Making of Luke–Acts*. An advanced and detailed study of Luke, well worth trying to master, is Hans Conzelmann's *The Theology of St Luke*, while a summary of recent work on Luke will be found in C. K. Barrett, *Luke the Historian in Recent Study*.

The possible influence of Deuteronomy on Luke (referred to on pp. 8 and 108) is discussed by Professor C. F. Evans in a chapter ('The Central Section of St Luke's Gospel') of the volume *Studies in the Gospels*, edited by D. E. Nineham. Two other chapters in this volume are interesting for the student of Luke: Professor G. W. H. Lampe on 'The Holy Spirit in the Writings of St Luke' and Professor C. H. Dodd on 'The Appearances of the Risen Christ'.

On the parables of Jesus it would be useful to read A. M. Hunter, *Interpreting the Parables*, and C. H. Dodd, *The Parables of the Kingdom*; and on miracles R. H. Fuller, *Interpreting the Miracles*, and Alan Richardson, *The Miracle Stories of the Gospels*. Two essential books on the teaching of Jesus in the Synoptic Gospels are T. W. Manson's *The Teaching of Jesus* and *The Sayings of Jesus*.

INDEX